Praise for

IN THE SERVICE OF YOUR COUNTRY?

"*In the Service of Your Country?* is a thoughtful presentation of military life. It is a valuable tool for those with little or no understanding of military procedures and promotion regulations; it is also a valuable tool for those considering military life. Those presently serving could gain insight into strategies necessary for attaining rank and pitfalls to avoid. Although it is a memoir of one veteran and his family's journey, it contains several life lessons that could be applied to daily personal and work life."

—Mary Ann Capuzello, English educator, AP and IB trained, retired high school and college level instructor

"LTC Paul Kirn's book, *In the Service of Your Country?*, is a wonderful piece of work that takes the reader on an educational journey. The reader gains insight into what it takes to sustain a twenty-plus-year career in the US Army. Interspersed with his stories as a young man figuring out his way through life are nuggets of wisdom shared from a seasoned veteran committed to his duty, served with honor, learned from his mistakes, and championed his own success.

"Along with sharing the personal details of multiple near-death experiences, there is guidance for how soldiers can stand up for themselves in an organization that demands you fall in line. Make no mistake, this book should be read by individuals navigating their way through their military service; however, the lessons can easily be applied to teenagers starting out in their first job or seasoned professionals working in the private sector. Any person who manages people, whether in the military or otherwise, will benefit from reading chapter 4 alone.

"What is Kirn's objective? It's three-fold. First, share a little bit about his life, which will hopefully make you smile. Second, teach a bit about strategies not widely known in the military, which will help to ensure you receive proper credit for everything you've earned in your course of duty. And third, that the wisdom imparted here can be used in your life, which will lead to memorable moments of sustained happiness, a common pursuit of all."

—Brian Kelly

"Your story is one of drive and perseverance. You fought for what you deserved and were awarded throughout your career for your hard work (in most cases). Your story should be read by all those interested in pursuing a career in any branch of the military. It may discourage some, but if they really want it, it shows what can be done. I am happy to know you and thank you for all you have done for us all. DARN!"

—Roger Mutch

"Whether military or not, this is a life plan for any career choice to begin a productive, fulfilling balance in one's life. *In the Service of Your Country?* is a great focused read on what it takes to succeed, especially for young adults who are lacking direction in their lives. Kirn's values, morals, and experience in military service cross over into everyday careers."

—Stefan Kaiser, publishing executive

In the Service of Your Country?:
How to Challenge the Military Systen and Win!
by Paul L. Kirn, CPC, LTC, USA Retired

© Copyright 2025 Paul L. Kirn, CPC, LTC, USA Retired

ISBN 979-8-88824-679-5

All rights reserved. No part of this publication may be reproduced, stored in a retrieval system, or transmitted in any form or by any means—electronic, mechanical, photocopy, recording, or any other—except for brief quotations in printed reviews, without the prior written permission of the author.

Published by

3705 Shore Drive
Virginia Beach, VA 23455
800-435-4811
www.koehlerbooks.com

IN THE SERVICE OF YOUR COUNTRY?

How to Challenge the Military Systen and Win!

PAUL L. KIRN, CPC
LTC, USA Retired

VIRGINIA BEACH
CAPE CHARLES

DEDICATION

This work is dedicated to my son, David Kirn, whose invaluable contributions (especially technical) allowed me to complete my effort. Also, I extend my heartfelt thanks to all the men and women who have served our country. Most important is the dedication of my wife, Lorraine, who survived with me for almost sixty-seven years. She, too, experienced/endured almost every aspect of this book. Because of this, I encourage you to read the foreword she wrote for your benefit. Hopefully, this book will help an infinite number of people.

Lorraine Kirn

TABLE OF CONTENTS

INTRODUCTION 3

FOREWORD 7

CHAPTER 1: Growing Up 8

CHAPTER 2: Beginning Military Service 14

CHAPTER 3: Protocol 23

CHAPTER 4: My Focus 27

CHAPTER 5: My Development 40

CHAPTER 6: KMC—Volcanic Activity 53

CHAPTER 7: More Quagmire 72

CHAPTER 8: The Battle Continues 82

CHAPTER 9: Promotion Achieved 93

CHAPTER 10: Perspective 106

ABOUT THE AUTHOR 119

INTRODUCTION

Though my experiences took place in the 1950s, 1960s, and 1970s, don't be dissuaded regarding its applicability today. Tweaks to the officer's rating system have and will occur, but those individuals powerful enough to create major changes believe that "the current system was good enough for me, and I got promoted, so why change it."

I know of nothing more important than deciding what we will do with our lives and determining how we will prepare ourselves to satisfy that goal.

History can be a great teacher, and learning from others' experiences can prevent the recurrence of problems while enabling one to circumvent difficulties or hardships that might otherwise arise. In this regard, this book contains a synopsis of experiences as they relate to a military career, and many of the conditions can be found in other walks of life.

You will follow my childhood and travel with me when I naively but enthusiastically entered the US Army as an eighteen-year-old American draftee. They selected me for attendance at Artillery Officer Candidate School, which I began soon after my nineteenth birthday.

Some salient guidance received from the Artillery Branch in Washington, DC—largely responsible for the equitable management of an artillery officer's career—can impact all officers. They pointed out that the following factors can be key:

- Need high-rated (outstanding performance evaluations) command times at all levels.
- Need to complete Command and General Staff College (or Armed Forces Staff College).
- Service in the Republic of Vietnam (not just adviser duty) would enhance my file—meaning that duty in any theater or area of conflict would be considered a plus compared to those who never served in these environments.
- Need important jobs—work at the general staff (G-staff) or joint staff (J-staff) level or in some unique, high-visibility, high-profile assignment.
- Avoid being rated and endorsed by someone of equal rank.

Life presents some unique circumstances, and I will share situations in which I confronted the Grim Reaper and rejected his invitation to the afterworld. One of these times occurred during a head-on highway automobile crash, which required brain surgery. Another took place when I was caught on foot in a flash flood and swept downstream. A third involved being caught alone in a vehicle that was covered by volcanic ash and pumice.

Documentary in nature, this reference can be a guide for all military officers in every military component, serving as a never-before-available road map.

My career took me to exotic places—Europe, Vietnam, Korea, and several locations within the US, including Hawaii. I was even selected to teach for two years at the US Army Engineer School. Entering the service with only three semester hours of college, I earned my undergraduate and master's degrees before I retired from active duty.

Being able to retire as a lieutenant colonel was an arduous achievement. I was forced to overcome the stigma of four consecutive efficiency reports (performance evaluations) that were considered below those of my peers and would have prevented my advancement in rank and retirement eligibility. Fortunately, there is an established appeal system allowing individual officers to correct erroneous, improper, or unjust evaluations. Each military service has an appeal process; however, successful appeals are rare. During my active military service, less than 10 percent of all appeals achieved the desired goal—a figure virtually unchanged today. My success rate was 75 percent. When the reader compares my three successful appeals with the one that was repeatedly denied, it may raise questions regarding the reasonableness and consistency of the Army's adjudicative process.

Any officer who believes their services were unfairly or improperly evaluated can glean invaluable data and examples regarding overcoming faulty evaluations. Though an appeal process exists, the availability of information outlining what could constitute a successful appeal is nebulous at best, a situation I have now corrected with this text. Throughout the history of our country, there were innumerable officers who were not promoted because their service history was not properly recorded. Now individuals can review their efficiency files and accurately address problem areas, if any, ensuring they can be properly compared with their peers for promotion, retention on active duty, and assignments.

My experiences with other military members led me to include samples of letters of recommendation and appreciation from general and flag officers. On my website, https://retltcpaulkirn.wordpress.com, you can review my actual contested efficiency reports. These can be invaluable to every officer. Thus, current military service members, those wrestling with navigating the corporate ladder, or anyone thinking about entering this country's military services should read this text for background; it can make a difference. My success in appealing faulty evaluations virtually mandates that every careerist should get this book and treasure it! It even briefly discusses similar conditions that one may find in a corporate or academic environment to assist those with other employment ventures.

The documentation in the appendixes referred to throughout the text was uploaded to my personal computer in the late 1900s, early 2000s. The original documents were destroyed when Hurricane Harvey ravaged my home in August 2017. These documents are provided for clarity and continuity and have not been edited by the publisher. The reader will note my Official Military Personnel File (OMPF) was lost (disappeared). More legible copies of the officer efficiency reports (OERs) for use in this publication were requested from the Department of the Army. On receipt, these were found to be no better (some worse) than existing documents.

These appendixes were meant to provide the reader with the exact documentation submitted by myself to obtain success. There are some punctuation/spelling errors in these appendixes (historic documents).

Readers can access these appendixes at www.retltcpaulkirn.wordpress.com, referred to herein by their corresponding page number in the PDF.

FOREWORD

Throughout his years of active military service, a great number of people suggested that my husband write a book and document the challenges he faced and overcame. For him to effectively convey, without bias, this perspective, which confronts every military officer, has been a difficult task.

Having experienced most of the events portrayed in this book, I know that every family, group, or individual contemplating life decisions can benefit from this book. One never knows how devastating the uncertainties of life can be; however, being aware of difficulties may enable you to avoid them. Should you be subjected to problems, know of solutions or possible courses of action that can correct or eliminate them.

Thankfully, my husband was blessed with the strength and manner that allowed him to survive the conditions he experienced. Somehow, he managed to live as a family man, perform his military duties (advancing from private to lieutenant colonel), and obtain his undergraduate and master's degrees, while overcoming factors that would destroy most military careers. He did what few, if any, have done before him. Before he was finally promoted to lieutenant colonel, he challenged four OERs, and 75 percent of his appeals were approved. This is a phenomenal achievement since the approval rate is only 5 to 10 percent.

A phrase my husband has expressed many times is this: "I'm here to help." By writing this book, he has shared the knowledge that can help a tremendous number of people. I hope you'll use it.

Lorraine Kirn

CHAPTER 1

Growing Up

When growing up, I asked the familiar questions, *What am I going to do with my life? How will I make a living? Is this really what I want to do? How can I pay for the training?*

To answer these questions, look to the **DARN** principle—discipline achieves results now.

- **Discipline**—this does not mean punishment for one's actions or failure to follow direction. This means possessing the regime to not be distracted, devoting efforts to learning and developing appropriate skills, adhering to respectable values, and having the tenacity to finish what you start.
- **Achieves**—establish goals and work to complete objectives.
- **Results**—the successful completion of your goal. Partial completion or an unsuccessful effort does not mean failure. But your direction must be modified to achieve a positive end. You can always learn from your actions (progress).
- **Now**—priorities must be established.

Merely implementing this principle does not ensure success.

Remember, part of discipline is tenacity. I'm reminded that Calvin Coolidge once said, "Nothing in this world can take the place of persistence. Talent will not; nothing is more common than unsuccessful men with talent. Genius will not; unrewarded genius is almost a proverb. Education will not; the world is full of educated derelicts. Persistence and determination alone are omnipotent. The slogan 'Press On' has solved and always will solve the problems of the human race."

Stumbling blocks may deter you from your goal. But there are many ways to achieve the desired result if you persevere and stay the course.

As an average Joe, I struggled with this. I was raised in a single-parent household (Dad passed away when I was eleven months old). In the ninth grade, I worked weekends at a toy store by my junior high school for fifty cents an hour. In tenth grade and on, I worked weekends at the grocery store across from my school. As a stock clerk, sacker, and carryout boy, I would double or even quadruple my weekly salary in tips. Looking back, though I enjoyed the money, I could have been better prepared to earn a living had I focused on my studies.

My academic accomplishments were not stellar. Since my mother was a teacher, I received a great deal of encouragement and assistance with scholastic problems—more than other youths. I can recall my mother commenting, "It will mean so much in years to come if you would only study and learn everything you possibly can—*now!*" How true that was. But who wants to spend all their time studying?

Additionally, during the football season, our Scout troop provided ushers for the Rice University home games. I thoroughly enjoyed this. This enabled me to watch the games without paying an admission fee, although I did pay a price. One Saturday before the game, I was participating in a game of chase, running thoughtlessly across the bleachers. Missing a step, I fell forward, striking the corner of a bench with my forehead, which created a V-shaped gash at my hairline. The next thing I remember is being in a doctor's office, where my wound was sutured with forty stitches (many internally). The doctor said, "I could have placed a silver dollar on his skull under the skin flap, sewn it up, and no one would know it was there." It was a significant injury, and I observed my blood residue in the stadium for some time before it finally weathered away.

Another injury occurred during an Explorer Scout outing. At dusk, our Explorer Post members were divided into two teams to compete in a capture the flag adventure. As the game progressed, I had captured the opposing flag. My mission was to get back behind our lines without being tackled by an opposing member. To do this, I had to jump off a five-foot cliff, into a sand embankment that was not being guarded by the opposition. Doing so, I experienced a sharp pain in my right ankle. The next day, following X-rays, the doctor told me I had a fracture. He treated my injury by wrapping it with an ACE bandage for three weeks. I moved about with the aid of crutches. Though this injury healed, it would present problems later in my life.

After I got my driver's license, I could use a family car—my mother's or aunt's. As a typical teenager, I was cited for speeding several times. My driving privileges would have been curtailed if I had not paid the fines with my grocery store earnings. This was the only law-breaking activity I was involved in as a youth. (Not true . . . I did experiment with smoking at twelve years old, but I quit after a few months when I realized I was burning through money.)

Being raised strictly by women, I'll never know how much I missed about my father. I do know, however, that my father cared for a healthy anatomy. Alcohol and tobacco use were repugnant to my father. Even without his presence, I decided those stimulants were not for me. My decision was reinforced by a newspaper clipping I found in his 1920s medical textbook, referencing a 1927 antismoking advertisement by the American Association for the Prevention of Tuberculosis:

A NEW ARITHMETIC

"I am not much of a mathematician," said the cigarette, "but I can **ADD** to a man's nervous trouble, I can **SUBTRACT** from his physical energy, I can **MULTIPLY** his aches and pains, I can **DIVIDE** his mental powers, I take **INTEREST** from his work, and **DISCOUNT** his chances for success."

This provides proof that humans are slow to employ available knowledge (change their ways) regardless of the harmful consequences. I'll always wonder what other tidbits I missed. How would my father's influence have affected my character or values? I'll never know how much knowledge he might have imparted to me if he had been around during my formative years.

Having seen how individual behavior can affect future opportunities, it is unfortunate that many youths rarely consider the consequences of their actions. There is no benefit that accrues from involvement in and conviction for criminal activity—robbery, breaking and entering, assault/rape, illicit drug use/distribution, driving while intoxicated, etc. Employers conduct background checks. Should one falsify an employment application, immediate termination will result. Government regulations preclude the hiring of anyone with a criminal record.

Following my high school graduation, I found entry-level employment as a mail clerk in a downtown bank. In their Trust Department, I met a beautiful lady who would eventually become my wife and life partner. Bank personnel encouraged me to become better educated. They even allowed me to attend college courses three mornings a week while working.

Deciding what I wanted to do with my life was not easy. My brother had a calling to become a Baptist minister (a focus that changed in his senior year at Baylor University). My mother and aunt, both college graduates with strong religious leanings, were thrilled with my brother's choice and happy to underwrite the pursuit of his undergraduate degree. I know they would have arranged to finance my college education had I been so inclined.

I asked myself, *How will I support myself? How will I provide for my family in the future? Will I go to college or vocational school? Is more studying really needed?*

I had enrolled in ten semester hours of basic courses at a local university, and I did not have a clue how I would make an adequate living.

A *black cloud* (the omnipresent military draft) hung over the heads of American males—or stared them in the face. It was a two-year obligation that could fall on my shoulders at any time. My opinion of the military was not high. Being part of the killing depicted in the glorified war movies was not attractive. The Korean conflict solidified my aversion to these *killing machines* (Army, Air Force, Navy, and Marines). Any interest grew dimmer when a neighbor (several years my senior) was returned from the Korean battlefields and buried with honors.

Here, as an eighteen-year-old beginning to venture into the world, I did not recognize or understand the patriotism that motivated others to serve in the military and make it a career. Nor did I even comprehend what sacrifices they had to endure. Though it was probably mentioned in school, I did not grasp that our military forces are controlled by civilians. It didn't cross my mind that the size of our active military is determined by Congress. Based on our current and projected needs, Congress authorizes a certain force level and the funds to support it. This force is controlled by direction of the president (commander in chief). He is assisted by his appointees (with congressional approval) who serve as the secretary of Defense, secretary of the Army, secretary of the Navy, and secretary of the Air Force. My naivete led me to expect that career officers and noncommissioned officers were a population of warmongers or other bloodthirsty types, maybe even sadists. I thought of the career military person as a trained killer.

As the sirens had beckoned and called to sailors in Homer's treatise, I too heard their call—"Uncle Sam needs you!" This rallying cry and similar recruiting efforts encouraged people to join the Army, Navy, Air Force, or Marine Corps. Thus, I volunteered to be drafted into the US Army for a two-year period rather than continue my college studies. My lack of focus was shown by completion of only one of my college courses (three semester hours). I hoped at the end of that military commitment, I would decide on a specific pursuit. It was my intent merely to satisfy a two-year service obligation, hopefully learn a skill, and become more mature.

Looking back, I would suggest that everyone consider spending some time in the service of their country. This would be especially beneficial for those who are not gainfully employed or satisfied with their present line of work. I'm not advocating that everyone should pursue a military career. However, if you are undecided regarding an occupation, why not opt to serve your country in some capacity for a few years?

CHAPTER 2

Beginning Military Service

It was an overcast morning in March 1957. At eighteen, I felt like I had climbed aboard the wings of an eagle. I was flown from Houston, Texas, to El Paso, Texas. When we arrived, the welcoming sun shined brightly as we loaded a military bus and were transported to Fort Bliss, Texas. I was to begin my indoctrination into the US Army. I expected to be in these surroundings for two years, after which I hoped to be better prepared for a civilian occupation.

I was pleased to discover that the Army (like all military services) has many opportunities. After we received the new inductee's heralded haircut, we completed a battery of aptitude tests. This provided insights into an individual's skills, capabilities, and potential. Test results enabled planners to develop future training plans and assignments. One's individual abilities (the primary factor) and desires (secondary consideration) allowed the proper slotting of qualified soldiers against job vacancies (requirements). Some marketable trades one might learn are electronics, communications, computers, logistics, maintaining automotive and/or aircraft equipment, engineering, drafting, driving, cooking, clerical, security, law enforcement, judicial, administrative, or medical. And now, the development process begins.

Paul Kirn in BCT

Everyone undergoes basic combat training (BCT) and learns the fundamentals of being an infantry soldier. No matter what specialty you possess, without regard to operating in any geographic area, the possibility always exists that you will have to defend yourself. As a trainee, you must be pliable and fit into a mold. One learns how to shoot a rifle and care for it. The teaching of hygiene and care for personal equipment is drilled into all new inductees. You also learn about responsibility and that you are a cog in the wheel—a vital part of a larger element. You must work cohesively with others. As Thomas Reid said, "The chain is only as strong as its weakest link." Each recruit is given uniforms, three meals a day, and a place to sleep. You are paid a modest amount while learning new skills. Medical and dental needs are part of your benefits package. How many other employers give you thirty days paid vacation annually?

The results of my initial testing showed mechanical/electronic aptitude. On completion of BCT, I underwent advanced individual training (AIT) to become qualified as an operator of a long range, early warning radar. The Army taught me to operate the AN/TPS 1D, commonly called the Tipsy Dog, to prepare me for assignment to an Air Defense Artillery site.

However, my high score on another test allowed me to apply for Officer Candidate School (OCS). Several of my fellow inductees also qualified, but only three of us elected to apply. Why did others elect not to pursue this opportunity? They said the following:

- "You'll have to serve more active duty time after you're commissioned."
- "Once you become a commissioned officer, Congress can always call you back to active duty if some conflict breaks out. You'll never be free."
- "I don't want the responsibilities they give you as an officer."
- "I hear life as an officer is really lonely. You can't have any friends."

Despite these comments, I thought, *You're so young. Another year of active duty won't really matter. I might as well get everything I can while I'm here.* So, I could apply to attend Infantry or Artillery OCS, and I selected Artillery. Again, my thinking was slanted toward the *killing* aspects of the military agenda—an idea I would later learn was not reality. I knew the infantryman was the first to be involved in hand-to-hand combat and would probably be found in the killing fields.

An artillery officer would be quite a distance behind the front lines firing artillery shells at the enemy in relative safety. I could see the artillery officer traveling between most points by vehicle while the infantry officer does most of his traveling on foot.

During AIT, I appeared before a review board charged with selecting applicants who would attend OCS. Toward the end of our cycle, classmates received their assignments at various sites throughout the world. It was not until a week after AIT completion that I received orders to attend the Artillery OCS at Fort Sill, Oklahoma. The class I attended commenced seven months after I entered active duty. While waiting on these orders, I remembered having to reimburse the Army for the cost of a helmet liner that I damaged during basic training. I believed that the Army would view that failure to care for government property as an act not worthy of leading other soldiers. How little did I know?

My next six months at OCS were the most difficult and demanding. The academic portion of our instruction was identical to Officer's Basic Course (ROTC and West Point graduates). Additionally, the program of instruction challenged our class with leadership, motivation, and physical training to ensure we were worthy of becoming commissioned officers. A new class of officer candidates would start every two months. Thus, one would begin as a lowerclassman (performing duties of a private). In two months, he would advance to middleclassman (performing duties as a sergeant). Then in two more months, he became an upperclassman (performing duties as an officer). Each level was constantly supervised/directed by the next level, and the cadre was always observing all levels. The demands were constant. Each candidate had to maintain academic standing under the constant scrutiny of superiors. Conditions became oppressive. This intentionally created tremendous stress. Wartime situations could not be created in the academic environment, allowing a candidate's actions to be observed/graded under battlefield conditions. Thus, the stressful environment at OCS simulates the strain one might experience on the battlefield and provides a qualifying measure.

At times, the academic schedule was extremely difficult. There was constant harassment from upperclassmen, and my need to study allowed me three hours of sleep each night during my first two months at OCS. Somehow, even with limited exposure to formal education, I grasped the mathematics associated with fire direction computations, the complexities of nuclear weapons fallout predictions, and the logarithms involved with surveying needs. Yet, many members of my class decided that completion of the designed program was not for them. It became apparent that those who voluntarily withdrew believed the *carrot* dangling at the end of the string (being commissioned a second lieutenant) was not worth enduring the program. Though I found the environment outside academia repulsive, I was not and am not a quitter. If the OCS staff believed I was not officer material, they would ask me to leave and tell me I failed.

There were fifty-six members in my original OCS class. It contained several candidates that had just completed BCT and AIT. There were a good number that had completed three or four years of service, plus some that had achieved the enlisted grades of E-5 (sergeant), E-6 (staff sergeant), and E-7 (sergeant first class). Thirteen graduated in the requisite six-month period, and I was one of them. My graduating class consisted of thirty-one members. Eighteen had started with earlier classes but were set back for an additional two or four months to improve their academic and/or leadership skills. We graduated and were commissioned as second lieutenants on April 1, 1958 (April Fool's Day). I never learned if this astrological date was significant, but I was proud of my achievements at age nineteen.

2nd Lt Paul Kirn

Then, it was decision time. The Army's basic organizational structure confronted me. Congress has established a minimum force level to satisfy our national defense needs, called the Regular Army. As worldwide activity threatens our national interests, Congress supplements the Regular Army level with members of the US Army Reserve. Even the National Guard can be used to augment this nation's active military forces. This supplemental force may be maintained on active duty at varying levels, depending on perceived threats or commitments to other nations. Correspondingly, this level can be markedly increased or decreased to satisfy conditions. Certainly, any decrease will result in reduction in force that can affect the careers of many.

As individuals joined the enlisted ranks of the Army back in the fifties, they could be readily associated with their service arm by their service number. If you were drafted for a two-year commitment, your service number was prefixed by the US. Had you volunteered to serve on active duty for three or more years (being guaranteed specific schooling or overseas assignment), your service number was prefixed by RA. Often, citizens joined the Reserve forces (becoming weekend warriors) to satisfy their military obligation and not be required to serve a two- or three-year active duty commitment. The service number of individuals in this group was prefixed by ER. Should you have joined the National Guard (another avenue through which you could satisfy your military commitment), your service number would be prefixed by NG. Today, an individual's social security number is now his or her service number.

In 1958, several years following the end of the Korean conflict, the Iron Curtain was firmly in place, and the communist threat from the Soviet Union was uncertain. This uncertainty was heightened by the Soviet Union's successful launching of the world's first manufactured satellite, the Sputnik. Yet the threat of hostilities was considered small and active duty forces had been scaled way back. All members of my OCS class had been commissioned as second lieutenants in the US Army Reserve (USAR). We were given the choice: Would we serve on active duty for two years or six months? Still uncertain about my future, I selected the six-month option. However, I was a draftee with a two-year service obligation (my BCT, AIT, and OCS time covered thirteen months). Thus, I was required to serve on active duty for another eleven months, until March 1959.

Upward mobility in the Army is controlled by the need

and vacancy into which one can be promoted—a condition found in most organizations. Imagine a pyramid is any massive organization, and the blocks therein are that organization's employees. Certainly, there are many employees at all lower levels. The proper performance of their duties supports those on the higher levels. As they gain knowledge and experience, they advance to higher levels, and new blood replaces them. The creation of opportunities at higher levels occurs when someone retires, transfers, leaves, or dies or if there is expansion/reorganization. Obviously, everyone cannot advance to higher positions. As one goes up the pyramid, the opportunities/needs are fewer, and advancement is more competitive. This emphasizes the importance of objective military performance reviews.

I can recall a time when promotion from second lieutenant to first lieutenant on active duty spanned a two-year period (that had been reduced to eighteen months when I was commissioned). I also recall that it was taking a first lieutenant from five to seven years to advance to the rank of captain. This was attributed to the smaller size of active forces that eliminated the more rapid advancement opportunities that existed during periods of conflict. Then, to become a major would require another five to seven years. Advancement beyond that level for a Reserve officer, whose active duty time was normally limited to a maximum of twenty years, did not appear realistic. Often, I would think, *If I can make captain and retire, I'll have done something with my life*. I knew I had an opportunity worth evaluating.

I realized, at that moment, that our military forces were concentrating on developing America's younger generation. Senior people were not being drafted, and volunteers were young. The rigors of combat demand that the vitality of physically fit, youthful forces be available.

Military services promote qualified talent from within. As

you find knowledge, develop skills, and prove abilities, you advance in rank or grade. Our military services are competitive. To ensure that deadwood does not hamper the development of others, the US Army has an up or out policy. Should someone fail to perform their duties, they will not be selected for promotion. If they are passed over by two selection boards, they will be released from active military duty.

The challenges before me were formidable. I knew that the percentage of officers on active duty in the Army without a college degree was likely small. There was no doubt that my job performance would be compared to college graduates. It was also apparent that my learning curve was just beginning. My pride required me to do the best possible job. Even though I would only be on active duty for eleven more months, I did not want to be an embarrassment. Thus, without realizing it, I began my military career in 1957.

CHAPTER 3

Protocol

Let me digress for a moment. There is more to a career than the daily grind. Though I'm sure you have encountered workaholics, there should be recreational pleasure complementing your existence. Do you desire to find the right "helpmate" and raise a family? Or possibly you would prefer to remain single and find your pleasures in life outside the bonds of marriage. It's unfortunate that so great a number of married couples find themselves in divorce courts. Yet, as you wander through life, will you find the desired love, flexibility, diversification, passion, satisfaction, joy, and happiness? This is like a career choice. How will you reach your goals?

There are no guarantees in marriage or career, and you must accept the consequences of your decisions. Finding and marrying the right person can enhance life's opportunities.

Anything is possible, and I'm reminded of a story I heard while growing up: Shortly after her husband's death, a widow attended a séance. The medium was able to establish communication with her dear departed. The widow asked, "John, are you happy now?" He was heard to reply, "I am extremely happy." The widow continued, "Are you happier than you were on Earth with me?" To her puzzlement, he responded, "Yes, I'm much happier than I was on Earth with you." The widow asked, "Tell me, John, what's it like in heaven?" "Heaven!" roared John. "I'm not in heaven!"

Seven days after I left Fort Sill as a second lieutenant, I married the love of my life. She has stayed with me, traveled with me, suffered with me, and supported me through it all with her caring and giving manner. Don't infer that I am reflecting on my life in the above story. I could not have found anyone more tolerant. Understand, though, that your spouse can be a party to circumstances that can beneficially or detrimentally affect your career.

There is a phrase that always cropped up when an officer or enlisted man experienced insurmountable problems associated with his spouse. "If the Army wanted you to have a wife, they would have issued you one!" (Of course, gender specific terms can and should be appropriately substituted at this point.) The manner in which you handle family matters (especially if they detract from or hinder your job performance) could be a critical issue.

Lorraine and Paul

Will your spouse demonstrate the type of character that will make you the envy of all? How will your life partner handle your social calendar? Will they be willing to help resolve the problems of your junior officer's spouses? Can your spouse handle your absences for a year or more when you are required to be away on a tour? You will be required to undergo schooling for weeks or months away from your permanent duty station. Will your spouse be able to comfortably exist without you? This may involve addressing difficulties that affect your children. Are they capable or prepared to handle these matters when you are away? If circumstances demand that you go to another duty station without your spouse, can they capably deal with all the relocation problems?

I understand that in many large organizations, individual mobility is an essential part of growth and development. Thus, the considerations I've mentioned are not unique to the military. They are, however, matters that should be discussed. At any point, unplanned circumstances can interrupt normal activity. Discussing courses of action will ease crisis resolution.

A situation may demand that you and your unit depart to address an overseas situation within a seventy-two-hour period. A member of your family may be critically ill, and you ask to be deferred from the mission. Your request is legitimate. Yet your job still has to be performed. If your commander cannot find a replacement, your duties must be distributed or reassigned, thus increasing others' workloads. Your failure to go with your unit may require reassignment, requiring the preparation of an officer evaluation report. Your valid reasons should have no effect on how your duty performance is recorded. But will your rating officer give you an objective evaluation? Can you be confident all recorded words and numerical scores are not tainted?

Be aware of etiquette and protocol. As you progress, you might find yourself serving as a general's aide, stationed in a foreign embassy, or working for someone in similar capacities. Be aware of universal standards. Subordinate your role and show deference to others by allowing senior officers, officials, or ladies to precede you into a room. There are many cocktail parties. These functions are not the place to conduct business. Should something be mentioned, simply say, "I'll call you for an appointment to continue this conversation."

The knowledge of proper etiquette can help in accomplishing things more quickly and easily. It will smooth the course of friendly gatherings and eliminate friction. Let me share some fundamentals. Do you know how an introduction should be handled? You should introduce this:

- Man *to* the woman.
- Junior officer *to* the senior officer.
- Younger person *to* the older person.
- US citizen *to* his or her peer from another country.

Formal invitations are always prepared, engraved, or written in the third person. If an RSVP is wanted, these initials should be placed in the invitation's lower left-hand corner.

Calling cards may no longer be in vogue. Your calling card was considered a very personal part of your first visit. It can, like that firm and confident handshake, create a positive, lasting impression. Several years ago, when you made your initial call to your commanding officer, it was appropriate to inconspicuously leave one of your cards for each adult member of the household.

CHAPTER 4

My Focus

One cannot imagine my state of euphoria as I, along with my new bride, went to my first assignment as a commissioned officer at Fort Hood, Texas (now Fort Cavazos). I felt like I was "off to see the Wizard" and had no earthly idea who or what I might find. Even with my youth and immaturity, I was not apprehensive about performing whatever task was asked of me. Here, I found myself joining an Honest John battalion, whose mission was to provide general artillery support to a corps. As a firing platoon commander, I quickly learned that working with troops and command assignments are valued stepping stones within the military hierarchy. Guiding, directing, and leading people to properly complete the assigned mission is what it's all about. The challenge is awesome.

Honest John Rocket

A policy I adopted at the beginning of my service was to never ask someone else to do something I would not do. I also quickly learned that no one is indispensable. Conflict can demand you work without all your people. I tried to learn or understand how the job of each person who worked for me was performed. I did not attempt to become as proficient as others, but it helped me grasp demands of those working for me. The people with whom I worked knew that I understood their duties and appreciated their worth. Because I approached my responsibilities in this manner, I found that my arrival or presence in an area was not dreaded.

Another factor that has always been important to me is *time*. Time, to an artilleryman, is critical. In periods of conflict, concentration of fire power from all units is essential. To obtain maximum effectiveness or lethality, it is planned to have artillery shells from all available weapons converge on a designated point or points at a specified time—the time on target (TOT). Achieving this TOT is accomplished by the coordinated efforts of each individual artillery unit. Since none of the units are geographically collocated, the flight time of each unit's artillery shells from their locations to the target is different. The wind and weather can affect the trajectory of a unit's shells and are considered in a unit's fire direction computations. Each unit determines when they must fire and gives their own command to fire to achieve the desired TOT.

Schedules should be maintained. Appointments should be kept. If conducting or attending a function or providing a service, plan and arrange to be there when it is scheduled to begin. No one should have to delay their efforts because of you. Everyone's time is valuable. Proper time management will enable you to do so much more than you ever thought possible. This mandates that you establish priorities and commit yourself to achieving them. Remember the DARN principle. Do you have the necessary self-discipline to make maximum use of your time? Will you also manage your time to ensure that others are not inconvenienced?

By now, it was readily apparent that the US Army was not the *killing machine* I had envisioned. I was being groomed to develop a versatile and broad approach with regard to my responsibilities. Not only was I charged with ensuring that the soldiers assigned to my platoon could perform their assigned duties, but it was necessary for me to teach them to maintain and safeguard their equipment. I acquired an appreciation of supply functions while experiencing the many facets of logistic support essential to one's mission. An axiom I learned early in my commissioned career is "You are responsible for everything that your men do or fail to do."

The Army educational structure is similar to that found in the US. One might equate BCT to their teachings through high school. Then, your AIT could be vocational school. Likewise, your basic officer courses could compare to undergraduate college courses while the advanced courses satisfy graduate level instruction. Attendance at Command and General Staff College and the War College would be training at the doctorate level. With this perspective, it is easier to grasp the different levels or hierarchies within the commissioned officer's ranks of the US Army. Initially, you are a company grade officer, holding the rank of second lieutenant, first lieutenant, and then captain. As you develop your skills and assume more responsibility, you advance to the field grade ranks and are recognized as a major, lieutenant colonel, and colonel. Finally, your demonstrated performance, experience, and schooling will enable you to progress to the general officer grades, brigadier general, major general, lieutenant general, and general.

Commissioned officers are taught to become chief executive officers (CEO) at different levels of responsibility. Obviously, everyone cannot and does not deserve to become a CEO. Yet, everyone is afforded that opportunity. Initially, you are exposed to challenges and learn necessary skills at the platoon level. Responsibilities are expanded, and you are given command of a battery (in the artillery) or a company. Should your demonstrated performance of duty warrant you to be promoted to the field grade ranks, you look forward to commanding a battalion—a position normally given to a lieutenant colonel. As a colonel, you might find yourself as a division artillery, brigade, or group commander. At the general officer level, you may be in command of an installation, a division, a corps, or an army. These are examples of command positions. There are many variations based on need. Thus, individual task forces or organizations may provide unexpected opportunities for any rank from lieutenant to general.

Even though the organizational concept in the US Army is directed toward developing its officers into jacks-of-all-trades, there are opportunities to become a specialist. As society has recognized the value associated with specialization, the military services have not ignored that worth. Without regard to the many career branches in the US Army (medical, judge advocate general, finance, transportation, adjutant general, etc.), you can become a logistician and focus on that field throughout your career. Computer services can also provide the right niche for you. Aviation might satisfy your yearnings for achievement. No matter your choice, if you apply your talents and intelligence, something worthwhile will transpire.

However, as a firing platoon commander, I quickly grasped and readily appreciated the value of the noncommissioned officer corps (NCOs—the backbone of the Army). They are the ones who know the ropes and rose to their respective ranks because of their expertise. It is my recommendation that any second lieutenant let the NCOs teach/share their knowledge and experience. The attitude with which you approach these veterans can dictate their response. Don't be aloof or ashamed to ask questions. You all have the same mission outside of the battlefield—passing your annual training test (ATT) and technical proficiency inspection (TPI) for those units having a nuclear capability, thus certifying that you can do your job.

Train with your soldiers to ensure that everyone knows their job. A philosophy I had and lived by was working *with* my men. There will be mistakes, but that's why you train. Learn from them; don't duplicate them. You've trained hard and gotten through your practice tests, and the ATT (or TPI) is a piece of cake. You were ready for it and passed with flying colors. Your personnel are elated. Pat your troops on the back and thank them for a job well done. The sense of accomplishment creates a feeling of self-worth. Your platoon has lived together, trained together, and gotten the job done. You've helped your unit complete their mission.

Your training is not over. Individuals will receive warranted promotions and be reassigned not only internally but to other units. Some will leave active military service, and you must redevelop or reconstitute that cohesive team. The training will be never-ending, and it can be enjoyable—it does not have to be a burden. All successful leaders surround themselves with those who can perform properly. Sometimes your subordinates may not come up with all the desired skills, but it is your responsibility to help them develop them. Your attitude regarding shortcomings can help them grow or be an inhibiting factor. It is inappropriate to criticize someone for an action you perceive to be faulty. If you identify a problem, ask someone if you can help them correct it. They may appreciate the offer and relish the help. Or they may thank you for bringing the problem to their attention but know that only they can correct it. Either way, offering your services will not be forgotten. You have created the thought that "I owe you one."

Repeating this training cycle can be boring. While keeping our forces ready to provide that active deterrent to aggression, other requirements will broaden your horizons.

The summer after I joined the Honest John battalion and got my feet on the ground, our unit was detailed to support the ROTC summer camp program, spanning an eight-week period. I was assigned to work as the assistant special services officer. In this capacity, I was the action officer on all recreational projects to include organizing the dance finale and decorating the post gymnasium for the function. It was a very successful program, and I had my first taste of a type of diversified activity that one will experience throughout their military service.

That fall, I came to appreciate the dental service. During a routine visit, the dentist questioned why my upper wisdom teeth were properly positioned, but no lower wisdom teeth were in evidence. X-rays showed that the lower teeth were present, but impacted and growing at right angles. I was told they had to be removed. They did so two at a time (upper and lower on each side). Removal of the lower teeth was not easy as they fused themselves to the jawbone. Yet, they completed the task with relative ease, and I did not experience severe discomfort. The dental care was just another personal benefit that I came to appreciate about my service.

Having begun to appreciate and enjoy what I was doing, I reflected on my future prospects. My job possibilities and ability to support myself and my wife if I left active military service were somewhat dismal. I was compensated on a par with commissioned officers who graduated from college or completed the military academy. *Why not stay on active duty and work on my college education? I could retire after twenty years of service at thirty-eight years old.*

So, I talked with my superiors, who were pleased with my services as an active duty Reserve officer. They recommended that I apply for integration into the Regular Army, which would allow me to remain on active duty beyond a twenty-year period, if desired. They also suggested I concurrently apply for extended active duty, which would still allow me to pursue my educational goals and remain on active duty should the application for a Regular Army commission be denied. To be integrated into the Regular Army, I had to have two years of college credits. I was administered a test, which I passed, and was told I would receive a two-year college level equivalency certification.

The Regular Army application was denied. Though no specific reason was given (only the blasé statement, "Other applicants were considered better qualified."). I was told I should complete my two years of college credit and reapply. Thus, pursuit of my undergraduate degree began. Later, I learned that one cannot be commissioned in the Regular Army until twenty-one years old. I feel certain no one below the Department of the Army (DA) ever thought to verify that this application from an active duty officer satisfied that requirement—being only twenty at the time. My request to remain on extended active duty was approved, enabling me to continue working in an environment I enjoyed.

After the ROTC summer camp experience, I focused exclusively on my duties as a platoon leader (or so I thought). Unfamiliar with the many functions that contribute to the smooth operation of a unit, I found myself overwhelmed when I was assigned *additional* duties:

Conservation Officer	Vector Control Officer
Training Officer	Area Improvement Officer
TI & TE Officer	Unit Recruiting Officer
Fire Marshall	Motor Officer
Safety Officer	Athletic & Recreation Officer
Postal Officer	Supply Officer
Security Officer	Bonds & Savings Officer
Public Information Officer	CBR Officer

Realizing that these duties could be a full-time job, I learned the value of delegating responsibility. Specific requirements associated with these individual areas can be addressed by your enlisted subordinates. Let them do the leg work. Should they uncover problems, you can become involved in whatever resolution is appropriate. Give them credit for their efforts.

Following another ROTC summer camp program, I received orders assigning me to an Honest John battalion located in Kitzingen, Germany (near the city of Würzburg in Bavaria). Government housing was not immediately available, so I was sent an address on the German economy by my sponsor. This allowed me to obtain approval for my wife to accompany me to Europe, which pleased both of us. During the next several years, whenever I received my permanent change of station (PCS) orders, we were able to enjoy what we made into a vacation when traveling between duty stations. Traversing the serpentine highways and byways of our country, we were instilled with pride and glad to be Americans, knowing our ancestors fought, negotiated, manipulated, and maneuvered (often losing their lives) to create and preserve our free environment. I have yet to find the quality and variety of services anywhere in the world comparable to those available in the US.

Thus, on the first of many "vacations," we drove from Texas along the Gulf Coast. Then, turning north, we wound our way through the scenic beauty of the Great Smoky Mountains National Park into the Blue Ridge Mountains of Virginia and then stopped to see many of the historic sites in the Washington, DC, area. From there, we went to New York (shipping our car to our European destination out of Philadelphia) and flew to Frankfurt, Germany. We traveled by train, an unforgettable experience, to our destination in Kitzingen, arriving in August 1959.

Prior to going to Germany, I was told that personnel assigned to combat units would be spending a great deal of their time in the field. I was assigned as a firing platoon commander, and shortly after my arrival, I participated in my first trip to Grafenwöhr (a major training area). Things were progressing well. On the first of October 1959, I received my promotion to first lieutenant. Later that month, I returned home with a pain in my right ankle after refereeing a battery football game. I thought I sprained my ankle, wrapped it in an ACE bandage, and ignored it. After a few weeks, the pain had persisted, with redness below the right knee and swelling. Medical personnel were baffled and placed me in a walking cast for a couple of weeks, hoping that immobilization would allow corrective action to occur. This did nothing for the problem, and just before Thanksgiving Day, I was hospitalized at the 97th General Hospital in Frankfurt, Germany, where medical personnel would try to diagnose my difficulty.

Exhaustive studies were run, and medical personnel decided that surgical fusion of my right ankle was necessary to correct my problem. Because the recovery time would be nine months, the procedure would not be done overseas, and I would have to be reassigned to a Stateside hospital. I had been in the European theater about three months, and my wife was seven-months pregnant with our first child. To prevent her from having to remain in Germany until after the birth, she elected to leave immediately and went to stay with her mother in Houston, Texas. At my request, I was sent to Brooke General Hospital in San Antonio, Texas. This PCS move was certainly not a vacation. I was transported in a US Air Force ambulance. This departed from Rhein-Main Air Base (close to Frankfurt International Airport), stopped briefly to refuel in the Azores, went to a commercial airport outside of Fort Dix, New Jersey, stopped at Keesler Air Force Base in Mississippi, and landed at Lackland Air Force Base in San Antonio. It seemed like an endless trip in 1960.

Here, a new team of physicians reevaluated my condition and did not concur with the diagnosis that had resulted in my reassignment from Germany. My present difficulty was related to the fracture of my right ankle during a capture the flag game before entering the Army. I was afflicted with a somewhat rare malady called minor reflex sympathetic dystrophy. When someone experiences an injury to any part of their body, the possibility of sympathetic nervous spasms subsequently occurring near the site of the injury and causing undesirable symptoms can happen. Various treatment modalities were tried to interrupt the nervous spasms, and the desired results were obtained.

My physical ills corrected, on March 1, 1960, I found myself assigned to another Honest John battalion stationed at Fort Bliss, Texas. Here, I assumed duties as the Assembly & Transport platoon commander, where the unit's principle mission was to provide support to the Artillery Board, conducting research and development activities designed to improve the capabilities of this free-flight rocket system. My platoon was responsible for acquiring, assembling, and transporting an operational rocket to the firing section for subsequent delivery to the target. Like the firing section, we verified the completeness of the rocket and warhead's circuitry and were scheduled to undergo our annual TPI on May 12, 1960. On May 11, I underwent an emergency appendectomy at William Beaumont General Hospital in El Paso—another unwanted hospital stay. Fortunately, my platoon passed the inspection, proving that no one was indispensable.

As a respite, my wife and I took long drives to scenic spots near where I was stationed. On Father's Day in June 1960, the three of us (our daughter, born in early March) packed a picnic lunch and ventured out to Elephant Butte Dam in New Mexico. At 3 p.m., heading back, we went south on the highway (before the construction of I-25) several miles south of Truth or Consequences, New Mexico. The road was far from level and straight because of the hilly terrain. Our three-month-old was asleep in her car bed, suspended over the rear of the front seat.

We entered a dip in the road and began to reach the top of the rise. Another car passed in a no-passing zone and struck us, head-on. Fortunately, the car bed somehow turned over on top of our daughter, and she was not injured. My wife was thrown from the car and suffered bruises and lacerations. Without room to maneuver, I had attempted to swerve to the right and caught the full impact (which totaled our car). I was knocked unconscious and do not recall any of the events surrounding this accident.

A person who observed the accident (but was not directly involved) was the vice president of an El Paso bank. My wife said he did everything he could to help until medical services arrived. He even left an old US Navy blanket that he wrapped me in—a blanket we enjoyed for many years. Regrettably, I never thanked him—I certainly wasn't able to at that time. Maybe someday he'll see this, recognize himself, and know that I truly appreciate what he did for me and my family. We were transported to St. Anne's Hospital in Truth or Consequences. Physicians told my wife that I needed greater help than was available there. They contacted William Beaumont General Hospital in El Paso, Texas, and my condition warranted immediate air evacuation for treatment. They were upset when, the next day, an antiquated field ambulance finally arrived to transport me for treatment.

By the time I arrived at William Beaumont General Hospital, I still had not regained consciousness. They found a laceration on my chin and noted that extensive dental repair was needed. There were abrasions to my hands and knees. There was a deep laceration on the ulnar aspect of my left wrist. They found a definite left-side weakness, which meant I was suffering from a blood clot or experiencing intracranial hemorrhaging. Brain surgery was scheduled, and they were not sure I would survive the procedure. Fortunately, the neurosurgeon relieved the pressure caused by a subdural hydroma (cerebral spinal fluid), not a hematoma. Had it been the latter, I might have been left in a vegetative state.

Following surgery, I remained in a semicomatose condition for three weeks. Still having no recollection of my situation or condition, I learned that my mother and aunt had come to my side. I understand they prayed for me, showed me pictures of my past, and read to me. My brother was in the Army—stationed at Fort Riley, Kansas. Receiving word that I might not survive, he visited me. I can't begin to understand the empty feeling he must have had when he left knowing that I was not aware of his presence. My brother had no assurance I would ever again function normally. Not long after my surgery, my wife said she stopped visitations by anyone other than immediate family because my mannerisms, verbal responses, and actions were bizarre. These prompted my visitors to laugh, which she did not appreciate. One day I awoke and recognized my wife. She made me aware of our traumatic events and told me that the medical staff was considering discharging me from active duty as a patient with permanent disability. Yet, over several weeks, to the surprise of almost everyone, I made a gradual recovery.

At the end of August 1960, I was released from the hospital and allowed to return to work. There was a period of mental adjustment as I tried to get back into the swing of things. However, my body didn't want to cooperate. My deep left wrist laceration had been sutured and shouldn't have presented future problems. Well, I experienced pain in my arm below my left elbow, accompanied by an unexplained redness near the injury. The minor reflex sympathetic dystrophy had again surfaced. This prompted medical personnel to interrupt the nervous spasms. I was hospitalized for an extended period. They surgically removed the scarring from the initial injury. They even found bits of gravel that were not taken out following the accident.

It was almost Christmas, and I had spent six months and eight days of 1960 in the hospital. No one could have predicted the medical complications with which I was confronted. Also, I was extremely grateful that I had received my full pay and allowances, I still had a job, and I had no medical bills.

CHAPTER 5

My Development

Hoping that my bouts with medical problems were over and to afford me an opportunity to completely recover, in December 1960, I was assigned duties as a battalion liaison officer (a captain's position). During the next three-month period, my attitude and duty performance persuaded my battalion commander to have me assume the responsibilities of the battalion S-2 (also a captain's position). So, in March 1961, I took over the security and intelligence functions of this unit and worked long and hard to learn all I could about the position and improve the efficiency of my section. In September 1961, a captain was assigned to our battalion, requiring that I be reassigned. My service as the battalion S-2 warranted the group commander (to which our battalion was subordinate) to have me fill a vacancy in his headquarters as the Group S-2. In this capacity, I was able to satisfy all demands.

Despite everything, I persevered. And in late 1961, after completing two years of college credits, I reapplied for integration into the Regular Army. This request was not favorably considered. I was not surprised, considering my recent medical history. Had I been evaluating my file, I too would have questioned this officer's long-term potential and recommended that his services be reevaluated at a later date.

I remained as the Group S-2 until June 1962, at which

time I went back to Fort Sill, Oklahoma, to attend the Artillery Officers Career Course. This surprised me because I had observed mostly captains and junior majors being selected for this level of instruction. At this time, there were two artillery career courses—a six-month course reserved for USAR officers like myself (conducted at Fort Sill) and an eight-month course (shortened from nine months) earmarked for Regular Army officers (six months at Fort Sill followed by two months at the Air Defense Artillery School at Fort Bliss). I had been selected to attend the eight-month course and was told that my performance of duty since being commissioned had persuaded the Artillery Branch that this was the appropriate option for me.

From July 1962 until February 1963, I attended the Artillery Officers Career Course. On October 1, 1962, with only three years as a first lieutenant, I was promoted to captain. My studies at the career course were cut short by two weeks because I had been ordered to receive six weeks of Vietnamese language instruction at Fort Bragg (now Fort Liberty), North Carolina, before reporting for duty in South Vietnam. Prior to proceeding to Vietnam, I settled my wife and daughter in Houston, Texas. Then, at Houston's Hobby Airport, memories flooded back as I prepared to leave for my new assignment. Several years earlier, I had flown out of this transportation hub when I entered the Army. Now, I was leaving the same terminal for parts unknown. My first stop was at the Las Vegas airport, where there was just enough time to donate several coins of the realm (quarters) to whomever owned the many slot machines that lined the airport passageways. Our next stop was the Seattle-Tacoma Airport (commonly referred to as SEA-TAC). Here, along with a full passenger manifest of military personnel, I boarded a four-engine turboprop passenger plane owned by Flying Tiger Airlines and began a long, monotonous journey to our Southeast Asian destination. On leaving SEA-TAC, our route took us over the top of the world (the shortest way) with our first stop in Anchorage, Alaska. There, I saw many picturesque snow-covered peaks formed by long-dormant volcanic mountains that stood majestically not too many miles from the airport's perimeter. From here, our commercial contract flight ventured out over the Bering Sea (in the northern Pacific Ocean). After many tedious hours, we found ourselves at Tokyo's International Airport. Because we were to be here for several hours, a number of us shared a taxi and visited downtown Tokyo (not long enough for anything more than a taxi ride). Maintaining our schedule (after many more tedious hours), our plane landed at Clark Air Force Base in the Philippines. Finally, after refueling, we began the final leg of our journey into Saigon, Vietnam.

On arrival in Vietnam, I was initially assigned to the Army Advisory Group as the headquarters detachment commander, I Corps in Danang. At this time, America's military presence in Vietnam was limited to approximately 15,000 personnel. Their purpose was to advise South Vietnamese forces in their attempt to thwart North Vietnam's aggression. When position requirements in this area were initially evaluated, it was determined that requirements for the detachment commander's position justified the experience of someone holding the rank of major. As a very junior captain, I was pleased to be afforded the opportunity of satisfying the requirements associated with this position. Here, I was responsible for the billeting of some 400 personnel scattered throughout the city, security, and the hiring of local nationals to perform labor plus maid service for our advisory elements. On top of these responsibilities, I was also the post exchange officer. For this function, I had one noncommissioned officer and three Vietnamese laborers to handle all the retail activities (bookkeeping/accounting, ordering, stocking, inventory, facility maintenance, etc.), resulting in a $25,000 monthly sales volume.

Immediately upon assuming my detachment commander's responsibilities, I learned that it had been common practice to requisition items sold in the Danang Exchange directly from the Saigon Exchange. They were then shipped to our location via a US Navy landing ship, tank. Somewhere between the Saigon Exchange supply warehouses and the Port of Danang, virtually all the luxury items (tape players, TVs, electric fans, phonographs, hair dryers, etc.) would disappear. Though responsible parties were aware of these thefts, the source of the problem had not or could not be identified, and the pilferage persisted. Thus, the military advisory personnel in our area of the country were being denied access to items readily available to most other military personnel in Vietnam.

To improve conditions and avoid the pilferage problem, I obtained approval to use the Corps' Caribou (similar to the Air Force C-123) and pick up retail supplies (including the luxury items) direct from Saigon. These resupply runs were coordinated in conjunction with other mission requirements on a monthly basis. This worked like a charm. The morale of personnel in the Danang area was given a tremendous boost. Items formerly unavailable were now present for sale. The second month I made this resupply trip, we had loaded the exchange goods on our Caribou. Our plane was sitting on the tarmac at Saigon's (now Ho Chi Minh city's) Tan Son Nhat airport, and it was midafternoon. The clouds were heavy with rain, and the ceiling was about 300 to 400 feet above the ground. Rather than delay our departure until the next day, the pilot decided to fly immediately under the cloud cover (to avoid the turbulence), heading east to the coast and then north to Danang. Because the cargo area of the Caribou can be confined, the cargo door in the rear of the aircraft was left open and positioned horizontally. I had placed myself on the floor near the open cargo door. When we were about twenty minutes out of Saigon, flying maybe 300 to

400 feet off the ground, I heard the firing of automatic weapons. Our pilot immediately pulled the nose of the aircraft upward as I observed bullet holes appearing undesirably in the cargo hold. We climbed out of harm's way and returned safely to Danang. When we arrived back at our home base, I learned that our pilot had been protected from severe injury by the reinforced steel plate installed beneath his seat. A bullet had struck the plate and ricocheted, grazing the calf of his leg. He was not aware of this injury until after we had landed back in Danang. Also, no vital part of our aircraft, nor any of our cargo, had been struck by the enemy fire. How fortunate we were. This was the first time I was exposed to hostile fire in Vietnam.

Throughout the detachment, I saw a tremendous need for improvement in many operational areas. Among these was maintaining proper accountability for the government equipment issued to advisory personnel. In this regard, I reorganized the supply accounting system to ensure an accurate inventory of some 200 memorandum receipt accounts. To improve conditions, I organized a detachment motor pool with taxi service for better vehicle use and established a bus route system for dependable transportation along the most used routes.

Halfway through my tour in Vietnam (as was standard practice), my duty assignment was changed, and I became an artillery battalion adviser to a South Vietnamese 105 mm howitzer battalion in their 2nd division, I Corps (from November 1963 through April 1964). The division was engaged in combat operations against the Communist Viet-Cong in the central highlands of Vietnam. I quickly established rapport with my counterpart, and we enjoyed an easy, friendly relationship. We had a feeling of mutual respect and confidence. While assigned to this duty, I frequently flew over operations in light aircraft to evaluate the performance of the battalion I advised. I really never thought about the danger associated with these flights, even though the aircraft in which I was a passenger was often the recipient of enemy fire. However, I'll never forget arriving at the airfield for a planned flight and seeing an Army pilot (captain) being removed from an ambulance helicopter. He had just been brought in from a "hot" area with a bullet wound in his left eye. For some reason, I never correlated that event with my job (thinking that could have been me). I also participated in the planning and conduct of the counterinsurgency operations in the division area, while ensuring military equipment provided through our Military Assistance Program was properly used and maintained by the South Vietnamese military. While I was advising this unit, most of their fire missions were restricted to H&I firings (harassing and interdicting fires—planned to interrupt the night infiltration of Viet-Cong units along routes identified by intelligence activities). I was impressed by the attitude of these South Vietnamese artillerymen and had no reservations with regard to their abilities. When I left Vietnam, I was proud of my efforts.

I would be remiss if I failed to convey that there was a break in the military demands on my services while in Vietnam. During the latter part of my assignment, I did enjoy an R&R trip to Hong Kong. I spent five days and four nights in what many defined as the paradise of the Orient. I stayed in a hotel on the Kowloon side. Having seen only pictures of the Chinese architectural masterpieces in this region, I appreciated digesting the magnificent beauty in this merchant's mecca. My opportunity to visit Hong Kong occurred after I had received my reassignment orders to the States. Thus, in addition to picking up a pearl necklace and earring set for my wife, I found a twelve-place setting of English fine bone china. This set was created by a manufacturer who enjoys international prominence. The US Embassy in Hong Kong was very obliging. They willingly arranged for shipment of my china to my new duty station in America using my reassignment orders. The set arrived without damage; however, on many of the pieces, the pattern was flawed during the glazing process. We fortunately found a merchant at a fine jewelry store near my new duty station who exchanged the flawed pieces without charge.

Prior to going to Vietnam, I had spoken with personnel in the Artillery Branch in Washington, DC, and asked what they recommended I do to improve my chances of being integrated into the Regular Army. They suggested I complete my tour in Vietnam and then reapply. I did, and in June 1964 (the third time's a charm) I received my Regular Army appointment as a first lieutenant with a July 28, 1962, date of rank. Being accepted into the Regular Army was critical to my remaining on activity duty until I elected to retire.

After the completion of my assignment in Vietnam, I found myself once again stationed at Fort Bliss, Texas. On arrival, I was assigned as the operations officer in the Control and Reporting Center of an Air Defense Artillery group. At this time, all artillery officers were considered available for assignment and capable of handling either field artillery or Air Defense Artillery functions. It was several years later that the Artillery Branch developed separate career paths (even distinctive insignia) for each focus. During this period (July 1964 through November 1964), I participated in a joint Army/Air Force exercise as the Army Air Defense liaison officer operating in the Air Force's headquarters. My responsibilities encompassed all matters pertaining to the HAWK missile units, which included displaying their alert status. It was necessary to ensure that an awareness of current air activity was known by the Air Defense Command Post and/or the individual firing batteries. Additionally, I was required to monitor and maintain a record of all Army Air Defense activity within the jurisdiction of the Control and Reporting Center. As usual, I put in long hours to ensure that all aspects of my operation functioned systematically and efficiently.

For some reason, a decision was made that two self-propelled eight-inch howitzer battalions would be located at Fort Bliss. In the fall of 1964, these battalions were placed under the operational control of the Air Defense Artillery group to which I was assigned. Then, in December 1964, I was assigned as a firing battery commander in one of these battalions. I was glad to be able to command a field artillery battery because my orientation (except for the few previous months) had been slanted in that direction. With this organization's nuclear capability (like the Honest John), we had to prepare ourselves for successful completion of ATTs and TPIs. My junior officers were recent college graduates who had entered the Army via the Early Entry on Active Duty program and had not been permitted to attend any branch qualifying course at Fort Sill. Encouraging these officers to enroll in Fort Sill extension courses and working with them, I was able to develop their professional abilities to the level of the Artillery Basic Officers Course graduates. Dealing with the problems associated with this command was enlightening. During the latter part of my year in command (ending in January 1966), my organization was in a state of flux, and we were relegated to performing garrison activities. Because our sister unit had been alerted for overseas movement, massive personnel transfers truly depleted my battery. Many of my remaining personnel's active duty periods had ended or were ending. Thus, maintaining our organization's equipment with approximately one-third of the authorized personnel was no easy task. Therefore, anyone who has been there knows full well the joys (and heartaches) of command.

From January until April 1966, I was placed on special duty as assistant G-2. This duty was with the Office of the Assistant Chief of Staff (G-2), assigned to the US Army Air Defense Command Center at Fort Bliss. Responsibilities were being expanded, and I was charged with the preparation of various studies having security implications. This included the preparation of several briefings. There was certainly no free time as I was also asked to prepare several policy papers under very stringent time goals, which required extensive research. In each instance, the time goal was met, and I received very laudatory commendations from the officers for whom I worked.

Then, in February 1966, I received orders assigning me to duty in Greece. My wife and I were very excited. We had applied for and received our passports when, in mid-March 1966, political demands had dictated a change in our military's focus. There would be a large increase in our military presence in South Vietnam. Thus, my orders to Greece were changed, and I was directed to report to the Combat Arms Branch of the US Army Engineer School at Fort Belvoir, Virginia. I would help train and prepare soldiers with an engineering focus to address our worldwide commitments.

In April 1966, I was the senior artillery instructor OCS, Combat Arms Branch, Combined Arms Division, Department of Engineering and Military Science, at the US Army Engineer School, Fort Belvoir (the Engineer Officer Candidate School had been created to satisfy the increased demand for engineer officers). In this capacity, I was responsible for organizing a previously nonexistent team of artillery instructors, which operated under the auspices of the Engineer Officer Candidate section of the Combat Arms Branch. Few assignments could have been more rewarding. I am firmly convinced that the best way to learn, know, understand, and retain any subject is to teach it. No instructor worth their salt will appear before any student body without being fully prepared and confident. Having attended a number of formal military training courses, I believe every instructor in a formal military setting follows that hypothesis.

Initially, our team revised the instruction, spanning four hours of counterinsurgency lessons plus an additional eight hours pertaining to military leadership. My goal was to present maximum content into a minimum time frame. This included the effective use of training aids to achieve student retention. Considering student enthusiasm, discussion, and participation, I have no doubt we achieved our desired objective. I also rewrote the combat operations examination that was to be presented to our students. To accomplish this, I performed a detailed analysis of questions to eliminate ambiguities in the test item construction. This included surveying the responses by use of the difficulty index, frequency histogram, and normal expectancy curve. I would then make recommendations for changes to the principal instructor for each lesson. Again, the desired goal was achieved. As the senior artillery instructor, I was required to monitor all artillery and related instruction. This was done to ensure continuity of instruction and coordinate class scheduling.

Though I do not consider myself an expert on the proper use of the English language, I know the unfavorable impression that its improper use can have. The ability to properly express oneself orally and in writing are attributes or qualities on which an officer is judged. I incorporated a brief lesson in one of my leadership classes. On the blackboard, I would place four magnetic signs that read as follows:

REOCCUR	**RECUR**
IRREGARDLESS	**REGARDLESS**

I would then ask the class (by show of hands) which is the correct spelling of the word that means "to happen again." Invariably, about one-half of the class would indicate that **REOCCUR** was correct without realizing that word did not exist in the English language. Even though common usage has recently made it somewhat acceptable, **RECUR** is still listed as the preferred spelling. Then, I would use the word

IRREGARDLESS in a sentence, followed by the same sentence but this time using the word **REGARDLESS**. The class would then be asked which reflected the correct use of the word shown on the board. A smaller number (but far too many) would select **IRREGARDLESS**, which is not a proper English word. It is important to verify the context of the terms being used to describe things. Inappropriate usage will grate on the nerves of any knowledgeable individual. I encouraged my students to check their written work, and think about the words they use before they talk. I didn't want them to be embarrassed.

It was obvious that I was performing my duties at the desired level. Having performed credibly as a captain, receiving objective performance evaluations, I received my promotion to major (along with my contemporaries) on November 30, 1966 (four years and two months after receiving my promotion to captain—slightly more than nine and a half years after entering the Army as a draftee). Yet it was during this assignment that I was confronted with some rating considerations of which I was not aware. Though my performance of duty to this point had allowed me to progress appropriately for my experience, I learned that all combat arms instructors (by virtue of being selected for this assignment) were considered the cream of the crop. It was an unwritten policy that if you did an excellent job while assigned this duty, your efficiency report would reflect that you had virtually walked on water. Just doing an average job would ensure that your efficiency report displayed that there were occasions when you got your ankles wet. My efficiency reports during this assignment were better (recorded higher numbers) than any prior reports I had received. I have no doubt that in selected assignments throughout all the military services, this idea is perpetuated. I never worked for the evaluation I would receive. I always performed my tasks to the best of my ability but now realized that many careers can be enhanced by virtue of one's assignment, just as it could also be hindered by one's assignment.

Since the Artillery Branch in Washington, DC, is responsible for the equitable management of an officer's career (and I was within a few miles of them), I solicited their guidance regarding my military future. Here are some points that were brought to my attention:

- Need high-rated command times (at all levels).
- Need to attend and complete Command and General Staff College (or Armed Forces Staff College).
- Service in the Republic of Vietnam (not just my previous adviser duty) would enhance my file—the message meaning that duty in any theater or area of conflict would be considered a plus when your experiences are compared to those who never served in these environments.
- Need important jobs—work at the General Staff (G-Staff) or Joint Staff (J-Staff) level or in some unique, high-visibility, high-profile assignment.
- Avoid being rated and endorsed by someone of equal rank.

With regard to these parameters, timing and the needs of the service are the deciding factors. A key position may become available after you were reassigned to satisfy another requirement that may not be as promising for one's career.

There may be positions with dynamic career-enhancing possibilities that are not filled because of political considerations. You might want to request a position vacated by a colleague. The career branch may respond with these caveats: "The needs of the Service demand that you be assigned to . . ." or "Sorry, Major Smith has already been selected to fill that need." A frequent comment is "Even though you possess the desired background and experience, others were better qualified." There is little any individual can do to affect their assignment at the DA level. You can voice your preferences and hope for the best.

In August 1967, the reassignment of artillery instructors at the Engineer Officer Advanced and Basic Courses dictated that I fill that void. As the senior artillery instructor, I examined ten courses to detect defects and establish teaching goals. I produced new programs to reach these objectives. These achieved commonalities and graduated progressively in content and time. During the latter part of my years as an instructor, I was concurrently the chief of a section, the principal and only artillery instructor and responsible for developing newly assigned field grade instructors. During this period, I standardized, maintained, and updated the Combat Army Branch's lesson reference file system of over 200 lessons. Time constraints also demanded that I organize matters, enabling my successors to rapidly assimilate all instructional functions in a limited amount of time. From here, in April 1968, I found myself on orders to Korea.

You will recall, the Artillery Branch had informed me that duty in Vietnam would be career-enhancing, and I personally requested my orders to Korea be changed accordingly. To no avail. I received the needs-of-the-service pitch and dutifully followed my orders to Korea. However, I was told that if my OER continued to reflect a performance of duty at the level of those I had received at the Engineer School, no assignment would be more meaningful than the other.

CHAPTER 6

KMC—Volcanic Activity

I moved my family to Houston, Texas. Then in May 1968, I boarded a commercial flight at Houston's International Airport heading toward my Far East destination. This time I traveled aboard a Boeing 707 with stops at LAX, Honolulu, and Seoul, Korea.

I was met by a liaison officer from the 2nd Infantry Division and transported to my new duty station with another Honest John battalion. This time I assumed the duties of the battalion's operations officer (S-3) in an artillery unit organic to the 2nd Infantry Division. Our division was engaged in active operations against an armed, hostile force in the Republic of Korea.

After evaluating the operational conditions in our unit, I completely reorganized my section to enhance its operational capability. Of primary concern was the need for a more definitive training program to replace the existing one. I prepared and implemented an annual training program that was not only more comprehensive and detailed but also easier to follow. This program was such an improvement within the division artillery units that they suggested other battalions use my program as a guide. My experiences enabled me to prepare many standard operating procedures with different focuses. Compliance with these guidelines far improved our battalion's operational capability. I planned and supervised the conduct of many field training exercises, which included both firing of live rockets and nonfiring proficiency programs. I was told that I was aggressive but tolerant and used a philosophy of firmness combined with understanding to greatly improve and develop my subordinates.

Major Kirn, Camp Snow (Korea)

Korea does not enjoy the tropical climate found in Vietnam. In fact, during the winter, we endured the heaviest snowfall and one of the coldest seasons they had experienced in almost thirty years. It is obvious that the weather may influence military operations, but it will not halt aggression. Our Army must be prepared to operate in any and all conditions. Thus, several of our training exercises were conducted when the Korean topography was blanketed by several feet of snow. Conditions were treacherous. When moving into any snow-covered area (bivouac or firing position), a vehicular guide (soldier on foot) would walk in front of each vehicle looking for dangerous spots. On one occasion, the guide in front of my jeep actually disappeared. The snow was almost waist-deep, and he had stepped into what we learned had apparently been someone's foxhole. We were cautious enough to ensure that no injuries occurred nor equipment was lost, which was attributable to climate conditions.

In December 1968, our battalion executive officer (my rating officer) had completed his assignment and returned to the States. His evaluation of my service at the time of his departure was on a par with ratings I had received at the Engineer School. Conditions from this point forward for the next four rating periods would defy the laws of probability.

You will recall my earlier comment that "A commander is responsible for all that his men do or fail to do." Well, in early 1969, an unforgivable sin for an artilleryman occurred. During a night exercise on our battalion ATT, the final firing deflection (adjusted by the low-level Windset system readings) that was set on the launcher resulted in a 100-mil (short for milliradian, a unit of angular measurement used to adjust firearm sights) error. When you consider the Honest John's destructive capabilities, an error of this magnitude would have horrifically devastating effects. Thus, our battalion commander was relieved of his command. Though he was a graduate of West Point, his career advancement ended on that day.

A new commander was assigned. Our battalion's capabilities were retested, and we passed with no difficulties. Because I was present throughout the earlier fiasco, it is possible that the new battalion commander for whom I was working subjectively assigned me some of the blame. My image had been tarnished, and all efforts to prove my worth were not given the credit I believe I was due. A copy of the OER covering this period, written by my new commander, is available at appendix I (page

125, website). For one who is not familiar with the Army's rating system, they would read the report and wonder why anyone would complain about its contents. Unfortunately, evaluations are so inflated that anyone receiving a truly objective evaluation (which is the intent of the system) will be virtually ostracized.

During my twenty-plus years of military service, the officer's evaluation reporting system was changed four times. Each time, we were told that too many reports were not being rendered with the intended objectivity. To overcome this problem, a new report (a new form with a modified format) was created. With mandates flowing through the chain of command, all rating and indorsing officers were enjoined to fairly evaluate others in accordance with the proper intent—nothing was to be inflated. The forms in existence during my period of active duty were DA Form 67-4, 67-5, 67-6, and 67-7. Each was created to eliminate inequities caused by inflated evaluations found in earlier reporting periods. To help you understand how the Army projected the anticipated ranking of its officers, I've extracted a potion of my earlier reports found on DA Form 67-5.

PART VI — OVERALL DEMONSTRATED PERFORMANCE AND ESTIMATED POTENTIAL (Read paragraphs 21f and 21g, AR 625-105)								
RATING	EXPECTED DIST OF 100 OFFICERS RATED	OVERALL DEMONSTRATED PERFORMANCE (1)			ESTIMATED POTENTIAL (2)			
		RATER	VALUE	INDORSER	RATER	VALUE	INDORSER	
a. OUTSTANDING	I	*	96-100	*		10		
b. EXCEPTIONAL	I I	*	90-95	*		9		
c. SUPERIOR	I I I		80-89			8		
	I I I I I I I I I I I I		70-79			7		
d. EXCELLENT	I I I I I I I I I I I I I I I I I I I I I I I I I I		60-69			6		
	I I I I I I I I I I I I I I I I I I I I I I I I I		50-59			5		
e. EFFECTIVE	I I I I I I I I I I I I I		40-49			4		
	I I I		30-39			3		
f. MARGINAL	I I	*	20-29	*		2		
g. INADEQUATE	I	*	10-19	*		1		
		SCORE						

The graphic portrays that in the expected distribution of 100 officers rated, the number of officers at the top is relatively small. Most people would believe that if you were rated as a superior officer with a numerical score between 80 and 89, you have done a very credible job. In the real world, an officer with that rating is considered substandard in comparison to his peers. To be promoted along with your contemporaries and considered for the more rewarding assignments and further schooling, you would have to receive outstanding evaluations and numerical scores between 96 and 100. Some evaluations in the exceptional area, with a 95 numerical score, might not be considered too damaging. You might pay attention to the rating adjectives, which can be meaningful in the narrative portion of the evaluation. If someone receives an overall demonstrated performance rating as an outstanding officer (96 to 100) and the narrative portion of their evaluation reflects an excellent job (correlating to a 50 to 69) in some areas, that officer's performance rating has been diminished. Had that officer's narrative portion of the report recorded that everything had been done in an outstanding manner (even a superbly outstanding manner), they would certainly receive more favorable consideration for opportunities. Some rating and indorsing officers may knowingly use these distinctions. So, the use of the words *effective, excellent, superior*, and *exceptional* in the overall rating scheme can have damaging effects. And, the use of these words for the desired results can be intentional or unintentional.

Before I left Korea, my new battalion commander shared a draft of the evaluation he intended to submit regarding my performance. We discussed my objections at length. He told me that it was on a par with evaluations he had received and had been rendered on others who had worked for him. The fact that he had been promoted to lieutenant colonel with comparable reports in his file convinced him that my arguments were without merit. He even recommended me for—and I subsequently received—the first oak leaf cluster to the Army Commendation Medal, attesting to the excellence of my service in Korea. I then talked to my indorsing officer, the division artillery commander. Sharing my concerns, I was hoping he would be able to convince my rater to alter his evaluation. He could not. (See appendix 1, page 124, on my website: https://retltcpaulkirn.wordpress.com.)

Leaving Korea in June 1969 with a somewhat heavy heart, I was resigned to the fact that, hopefully, this one report wasn't really that damaging. I was looking forward to my new assignment in Hawaii. Like all who have never been there, I went with great anticipation to enjoy the niceties of that island paradise.

On the way back to the *mainland* (a term those in Hawaii call the rest of the States), our flight stopped briefly on the islands of Okinawa and then Guam before arriving in Honolulu. As the appropriate authorities in USARHAW (US Army, Hawaii) knew I was being assigned, they requested I stop by to learn if their thoughts concerning my assignment were satisfactory. After a brief orientation, I was told they would like me to fill a soon-to-be vacant position on the Big Island. Here, I was to be the commanding officer of Kilauea Military Camp (KMC—a lieutenant colonel's position), which was considered a command position. I could not have been more pleased. Field grade officers throughout the Army are clamoring for command assignments because of their value in favorably influencing promotion selection boards.

I was flown to view my proposed assignment at this Joint Service Rest and Recreation Center. The military services in Hawaii had determined a need for a recreation facility to be enjoyed by all active and retired military personnel and their dependents. On space leased from the Department of the Interior, this facility is found in the Hawaii Volcanoes National Park at an altitude of approximately 4,000 feet. By agreement, the Army provides the commanding officer and primary support for this activity. His executive officer is provided by the Air Force, plus drivers for the tour buses. The Navy provides personnel requirements for the food service (cafeteria) to include the provisions sales room (a small commissary); in addition, the Marine Corps satisfies the need for fire protection and security personnel.

At KMC, all guests (regardless of rank) are considered VIPs and are treated accordingly. The challenge that I saw when I initially visited the camp was exciting. My future couldn't have appeared brighter, and the misgivings I harbored on leaving Korea were completely obscured. Though I really was in an airplane between Hawaii and Houston, where I again joined my family, the opportunities I saw at KMC made me feel like I was walking on air.

One will find that the Army (as all services) moves personnel between duty stations using all modes of transportation to ensure that no carrier is slighted. For the most part, movement is by air transport. However, recognizing that the most anyone could do is decline, I requested our family be sent to Hawaii by ship. Surprise, surprise! My request was approved in July 1969. We drove to California, where we would embark for Hawaii. This time, we crossed the vast open ranges of Texas, passing through El Paso. From there, we went across the lower reaches of New Mexico and Arizona, into Phoenix, and turned north to visit the spectacle of the Grand Canyon. Our next stop was Disneyland. Every child, even those *children* in parent's bodies, have a great time in this fun world. Moving on to our midpoint, we veered slightly from the coast to view the magnificent redwoods in Yosemite National Park. It was an awe-inspiring experience. Driving through the base of one of these beauties was also an adventure. To have viewed these sequoias, towering hundreds of feet in the air and reaching for the heavens, was certainly something I'll always be glad I saw. Arriving next in San Francisco, we shipped our car to the Big Island and boarded the SS *Lurline* for our cruise to Hawaii. A picture of this magnificent cruise liner can be seen below. Though this ocean voyage occurred more than fifty years ago, our accommodations were very comfortable and satisfying.

SS Lurline—Matson Lines Luxury Liner

How could one ask for more? The weather was beautiful, and we were leaving to sail out into the Pacific (the *peaceful*) Ocean. That first evening, we were served a five-course dinner fit for a king. As we left the dining hall, I deposited my dinner in an ashtray stand on one of the stairwell landings. I was fairly miserable for the next several hours, and my wife and daughter laughed and enjoyed my situation. How could I have gotten seasick on this huge ship? Even though I knew I was subject to motion sickness, especially on small aircraft, travel on large planes had never been a problem. So, venturing out into this *peaceful* ocean aboard this huge vessel should not present any difficulties—ha! I soon learned that the ocean swells can oftentimes upset the heartiest of souls.

The next morning, everything was smooth sailing. The rest of our five-day trip was pure pleasure. I thoroughly enjoyed all of my meals. The excellence attributed to shipboard cuisine is not exaggerated. The variety of daily activities for the passengers was impressive. Though I'm not a skeet shooter, I tried my hand at their offering. We were given chances to see who could drive a golf ball the greatest distance. It was obvious that I didn't excel at this activity either. There was shuffleboard, swimming, table tennis, dancing, and slot machines. Our trip was relaxing and enjoyable. A postcard from this vessel reflects that it has spacious and distinctly designed public rooms and staterooms, bragging that they were the finest in sea-travel luxury. This completely air-conditioned liner accommodated 761 passengers—all in first class. It was 632 feet in length and could achieve a speed of 22 knots. This mode of travel is not restricted to officers. A US Navy chief petty officer (being assigned to duty at Pearl Harbor) along with his wife and three children (two daughters and one son) shared our table en route to Hawaii. When we arrived in Hawaii, my wife, daughter, and I spent a couple of days on Oahu before we went to the Big Island for our new adventure.

Major Kirn, CO, KMC

Though all military services are involved in the operation of KMC, I am convinced that only a relatively small percentage of people who are authorized to take advantage of its services are even aware of its existence. A stay at KMC is a real vacation bargain. During my tenure, for a small fee (which covered room and board, guided tours, and transportation to and from the airport), graduated according to one's rank, you could truly have the time of your life. I believe the same is still true today.

On the Big Island where KMC is found, one can experience almost any desired climatic condition. During virtually every winter season, you will find snow on Mauna Kea (the tallest island mountain in the world). Also, on this island is a cattle ranch—one of the world's largest and finest. There are luscious tropical forests, beautiful beaches, and a relaxed atmosphere where everything doesn't have to be done today. The camp itself is within the Hawaii Volcanoes National Park, where you will find many of the world's most active volcanoes. Nestled on the slopes of Mauna Loa (where snow is also occasionally seen during winter months), KMC's temperature seldom exceeds 80 degrees Fahrenheit. As a guest, you are encouraged to vary your dress according to the activities in which you participate. For most activities, aloha shirts, shorts, or slacks are appropriate. Heavy shoes are recommended for hiking. The cool weather found from October through March suggests you should bring a raincoat, lightweight coat, or sweater. Relaxing in informal wear, including muumuus, in the evenings is a recipe for vacation.

To ensure that your stay is enjoyable, there is a small post exchange. In the recreation lodge, you can rent automobiles, golf clubs, and bicycles. Baby strollers and alarm clocks are available. Here you will also find a gift shop where guests may purchase souvenir items. There are pool tables, Ping-Pong tables, playing cards, shuffleboard, and other indoor games. Equipment is available for outdoor activities—tennis, basketball, and volleyball. A laundry and dry-cleaning service are available, and an eighteen-hole golf course is in walking distance. They don't actually get "first run" showings of motion pictures, but a theater is available for nightly cinematic adventures. A library is available for those who want to use it and even a clean, well-equipped nursery should you want to take advantage of it. You will find a six-lane bowling alley, a beauty shop, a barber shop, and a dispensary. On weekends and Holy days, Catholic and Protestant services are held in the chapel.

Five days a week, KMC guests are invited to participate in guided tours arranged around points of scenic and historical interest. Some of the tours will take guests quite a distance from the camp. On these days, guests will be brought and served a fabulous lunch at a prearranged site: Akaka Falls, Liliuokalani Gardens, Coconut Island, Kilauea Caldera, Hawaii Volcanoes National Park, the Painted Church, Kaimu Black Sands Beach, Rainbow Falls, and Mauna Loa Orchids—one of the Big Island's fastest growing industries and a macadamia nut orchard.

Kilauea Volcano

Wanting to improve my knowledge base as the KMC commander, I found myself experiencing an extensive amount of volcanic activity that I was privileged to see and record on 8 mm film. I prepared a presentation on how the Hawaiian Islands were formed that has been shared with several groups. It consists of a twenty-eight-minute video presentation (can be viewed on https://retltcpaulkirn.wordpress.com), which I narrated, and includes volcanic sounds. The activity is from the Aloi-Alae vent, which occurred in 1969 and 1970.

In my narrative, I explain that the Hawaiian archipelago stretches approximately 2,000 miles across the north central Pacific and consists of 124 islands, islets, and atolls. These are actually the peaks of a tremendous mountain range rising from the ocean floor. In this archipelago, the eight principal islands are commonly known as the Hawaiian Islands. The largest of this island grouping, Hawaii, was formed exactly like all the rest.

I then begin with a sequence showing the now extinct Mauna Kea, "white mountain." Then I moved up the east slope of the largest single mountain mass in the world, a panorama of Mauna Loa, "long mountain." This mountain extends upward from sea level some 13,690 feet and has a volume of approximately 10,000 cubic miles. When I initially made this presentation, I would inform listeners that Mauna Loa last erupted in 1950 (it has now erupted again), sending lava down its western slopes to the sea along the Kona coast.

Moving back to another view of Mauna Kea, I let my audience know that it is the highest island mountain in the world, towering 13,796 feet above sea level. Some 18,204 feet of this mountain are below sea level, making it 32,000 feet tall (that portion above sea level is nine times the height of New York City's Empire State Building).

Having observed two of the five mountain masses on the island of Hawaii, I now provide a view down the flanks of a third mountain mass, the Kilauea volcano. The area shown is between Aloi and Alea craters down the Puna rift zone. Kilauea is considered the world's most active volcano, and looking at the desolate area on the film footage will aid in your understanding of how all islands in this chain were formed. Actually, lava will seep or gush from craters atop the volcano or from vents that erupt sporadically in the same general vicinity. This lava will flow in layers, forming new land on top of old. Slowly, mountains are formed to the height of Mauna Kea and Mauna Loa, just as an acorn will become a mighty oak. Finally, all growth will cease.

My audience is told that molten activity broke out in the region shown on film on February 22, 1969, severing the Chain of Craters Road, which once connected the Hawaii Volcanoes National Park with the Kalapana area of the island. I moved up to the brink of the Aloi-Alae vent, where activity began anew on May 24, 1969. Looking down less than twenty feet away beneath the surface of the earth, magma was boiling at approximately 2,200 degrees Fahrenheit. Magma is the molten or semimolten natural material from which all igneous rocks are formed. The constant bubbling and turbulence within the vent are caused by the escaping or release of many gases or vapors. Of these vapors, steam is most abundant. Chlorine and sulfur and various compounds of these elements are among the commonest fumes escaping from volcanic vents. Carbon dioxide gas is also common. Many of these gaseås are poisonous, and it can be dangerous to approach the craters or cracks from which they issue. I call attention to the dark spots on top of the rolling magma. This is nothing more than an area on the magma's surface that has been exposed to the air for more than a few seconds and has cooled. It then rolls back beneath the surface. Once magma is released from the caldera, either through the main vent or a fissure in the earth's crust, and begins to solidify, it is lava. There are two types of lava flows: "Pahoehoe," a smooth, sinuous, rope type and "Aa," a coarse, very rough, chunky type.

Having moved back to a much safer vantage point (six-tenths of a mile southwest of the vent), my viewers observe a ball of molten lava, which appears as a rising or setting sun. This activity took place in early December 1969 and was created by excessive steam pressure, which is the principal force present during eruptions. It was classified as interphase activity; a phase of activity is defined by US Geological Survey personnel as any activity in which the rate of volume of magma thrown out of a vent is more than 1,000,000 cubic yards per hour. The bubbling lava is being emitted from the same vent as the panorama of the Aloi-Alae vent.

The next sequence captured the beauty of the thirteenth phase of vent activity, which occurred on December 30, 1969. When photographing this activity, I was standing almost due west of the vent, next to the Pauahi double crater roughly 1.6 miles away as the crow flies. Without pictures, it's difficult to imagine the beautiful colors within the fan of molten lava, which, at this time, was being hurled approximately 1,300 feet in the air. As of that time, the highest lava fountains measured from any of the Hawaii volcano eruptions occurred in December 1959, when the Kilauea Iki eruption reached a height of 1,900 feet. This particular phase lasted about eight hours, and during this period, nearly 14,000,000 cubic yards of lava were thrown from this vent. In a few years, depending on rainfall and climatic conditions, this lava could be covered with vegetation and ready for cultivation. It's easy to see why this state is sometimes termed the fastest growing state, not only in population but also in area. Frequently, the lava from these eruptions flows into the sea, adding new land area to the state.

Once again, I moved back to my earlier location six-tenths of a mile southwest of the vent, a much closer view of the molten lava spray. Here, the lava spills over the *pali* (cliff—edge of a crater) into the crater, whose depth is about 150 feet. In May 1970, lava oozing through lava tubes completely filled this crater and obliterated it from view. Visiting this area today, one would never know it once existed. The heat at this point (six-tenths of a mile away) is quite intense. Listening to the rhythmic roar associated with an eruption of this type is quite awesome. While photographing these sequences, I was seated in a station wagon. Bits of molten lava and pumice almost completely covered the vehicle during the short period I was there. This is certainly an area in which the public is not allowed during a phase of activity; it is dangerous. In fact, the entire vehicle had to be repainted and the front window replaced after I left.

Additional footage shows the volcanic fountains reaching upward to near 1,600 feet. Looking closely at the base, the lava is being thrown from two separate but collocated vents and coalesces as it finds its way upward. I was able to capture a very unusual phenomenon—a thermal whirlwind, which is nothing more than bits of pumice being picked up near the vent by wind eddies. The dangers associated with this type of natural activity are legendary. As a youth, I often heard tales (which the soothsayers swore were true) about the destructive force of a tornado or whirlwind. The uncontrollable winds churning within these dreaded scourges of nature are said to have the capability of driving a broom straw through a tree.

The heat was becoming unbearable, and I moved back to the Pauahi double crater a little more than a mile and a half away. Again, you can still see the thermal whirlwind silhouetted against the volcanic fountain of molten lava. You can also spot a private aircraft flying across the screen whose occupants are literally getting a bird's eye view. A towering volume of noxious smoke extends upward, covering several square miles. I've always wondered what kind of legislative control the environmentalists would propose to correct this problem.

That activity stopped as abruptly as it began. Once again, all is quiet. I doubt if one would recognize the region I photographed if you visited it today. Even before I left the Big Island, a good amount of activity created another volcanic hill, Mauna Ulu, "growing mountain." Now, instead of a flat area, you would find a smoking volcanic mountain, which grew to 300 feet in September 1970.

Returning to my other duties, I had to transition from using survival skills to employing leadership skills. Anyone who has managed a large operation knows the difficulties associated with maintaining that operation. Training and developing workers in an always changing personnel environment is a demanding challenge. Creating and retaining a working atmosphere that motivates your workforce to always do their *best* is also an awesome responsibility. I really loved my job and relished the responsibilities. Because of this camp's isolated location and knowing the history of its previous commanders, I thought there might be a possibility that I could spend my entire Hawaiian tour (three years) at this location. I knew things were going well, and I had yet to hear a critical word regarding my duty performance at KMC. However, my career aspirations were once again shattered when I received a copy of the OER written by my rating officer, who was being reassigned in May 1970 (appendix II, page 128, on my website).

When I read this report, I felt betrayed. I flew to Oahu, and discussed my evaluation with my rating and indorsing officers. I could not obtain any justification for the evaluation. I visited with the colonel, who was the USARHAW's inspector general. He had previously inspected KMC during my tenure for compliance with applicable directives and was pleased with his findings. He also strongly disagreed with my evaluation and said he would gladly guide me to have this report removed from my file (a rarely achieved accomplishment). Under his tutelage, I discovered the avenue by which an invalid OER could be removed from one's file. However, there are no specifics with respect to what information would allow any report to be modified or removed. The established preparation process demands that your rating, indorsing, and reviewing officers follow meticulous guidelines. Thus, in its final form, the OER is considered a sacrosanct document. You must decide what *evidence* will enable you to combat an evaluation. The uniqueness associated with the rating of individual military officers does not allow for the creation of a standard rebuttal criterion. Obviously, every case will be different, and you must decide the appropriate approach for your situation.

One's efforts to overcome a *faulty* or *erroneous* evaluation cannot interfere with the performance of their assigned duties. Your attitude is crucial. If you are thought to be carrying a chip on your shoulder, getting help will not be easy.

Always the optimist and now aware that the Army provided a way to overcome rating inequities, I believed I could prevail. Thus, in August 1970, I submitted my initial attempt (appendix III, page 132, website) to eliminate from my file what I considered an invalid rating, spanning June 11, 1969, to May 12, 1970. One might question why I didn't immediately request to be reassigned. There were two reasons. I decided I would be able to eliminate this report. By doing so, it would prevent the preparation of similar reports during my stay at KMC. And my wife was pregnant with our son, born in Hilo, Hawaii, in early August 1970. A change of assignment would have required I be relocated to Oahu.

Soon after submission of the original rebuttal information, I was informed by the Field Artillery Branch that an officer who appeals his OER with no evidence other than his statement has little chance of winning. A reclama should be accompanied by substantive evidence, which is defined in AR 623-105, OER, as "Statements from third parties who were in official positions which enabled them to observe directly the manner in which the appellant performed his duties during the rated period." This was soon followed by twenty-five letters of support from a major general (the USARHAW commander) and a rear admiral (the commandant Fourteenth Naval District, commander, Hawaiian Sea Frontier, and commander, Naval Base, Pearl Harbor) (appendix IV, page 173, website). To obtain these letters, I showed or provided a copy of my OER. These officers knew the rating system was skewed and would ruin my career. The letters of support from enlisted personnel were willingly prepared. The commanding general (4 stars), US Army, Pacific (USARPAC), also disagreed with the evaluation and told me he would provide a letter of support. He stayed at KMC during my tenure. Several letters of appreciation from guests at KMC came through his office and were endorsed by him. Additionally, the commanding general (2 stars), USARHAW, charged with the responsibility for KMC, agreed to provide me with a letter of support.

Though I was willing to remain at KMC, in September 1970, I learned I was being reassigned. Knowing the rapport I had established with the people of the Big Island, I did not want them speculating about my sudden and unexpected departure. At the next rotary meeting, I discreetly shared the circumstances I was experiencing. I also informed them of the support I was getting. Following this meeting and without my knowledge, one of the rotary members, associated with a local radio station, broadcasted what I had discussed. This radio broadcast was monitored on Oahu and reported to the commanding general, USARPAC. I never learned exactly what was said on the air; however, following that broadcast, USARPAC's commanding general informed me that no letter of support would be forthcoming from him. Though I can't confirm it, responsible parties must have believed that I had damaged the Army's image and publicly criticized that institution—bit the hand that fed me.

Because of this incident, I had apparently fallen out of favor. In early October 1970, I was reassigned to Oahu. This required the preparation of another OER—a new rating officer, the same indorsing officer whose judgment I had already questioned. Thus, an evaluation that was even more damning was prepared and submitted (appendix V, page 209, on my website). In addition to performing my daily duties, I once again found myself collecting data and preparing my challenge for another unfair report. Later, I will pinpoint one portion of the rating officer's evaluation that was changed, I believe, due to the indorsing officer's influence.

CHAPTER 7

More Quagmire

Arriving on Oahu, I was assigned duty as a field artillery adviser to a Hawaii National Guard 105 mm howitzer battalion. I was privileged to associate with quality professionals; it was rewarding. I intended to do the best possible job.

It is a common hope when one moves that any unfavorable image will be left behind, and they will begin with a clean slate. As big as the Army is, you would think this would be a reality. Unfortunately for me, this was not the case. My new duty station was in the vicinity of Diamond Head—the Gibraltar of the Pacific. Here, my new rating officer, a lieutenant colonel, was friendly with the lieutenant colonel (located at Schofield Barracks) who rendered my second evaluation at KMC. At some point, they discussed my situation. Their mutual respect and credence created an environment that would not allow me to be rated objectively.

For the next year, I worked an exhausting schedule, dedicated to performing my job so well that I would receive an outstanding evaluation. It is extremely rare to overturn or eliminate an unfair evaluation. History has shown that because of the existing safeguards to ensure the proper preparation of an OER, errors rarely occur that warrant modification (this is the position espoused by the hierarchy). Knowing this, you cannot imagine my feeling of elation when, in March 1971, I was notified by the DA that my appeal of my first report at KMC had been approved (appendix VI, page 212, website). I'm convinced the key to this favorable resolution was the volume of third-party letters of support headed by the USARHAW commanding general. This was credible evidence that offered sufficient information to support my appeal. That period has now been declared a nonrated period. By policy, that OER and related correspondence filed with my appeal must be removed from my official records. The way my file was purged would create problems. I had provided copies of the letters of appreciation and commendation that I received at KMC. These were to be included in a permanent part of my official file. Though I had attached copies of these letters to my rebuttal, which should and would be removed on approval of my appeal, I later learned that most of the other letters were also removed. This caused difficulties later.

Remember, actions associated with rebutting an OER must be considered ancillary to your assigned duties. I would spend nights and weekends uncovering details associated with rebutting any report. Don't be misled. For me, the Army was never a nine-to-five job. These appeal activities would be arranged around my other responsibilities. My priorities were given first and foremost to my present duties and academic pursuits. Realizing that my initial rebuttal had been approved, my morale was certainly buoyed, and my expectations were high when I submitted my rebuttal of the second OER in April 1971 (appendix VII, page 214, website). In the rebuttal, I included a copy of my rating officer's draft OER, given to me prior to its finalization and specific reference to the changes that were probably caused by undue influence.

Having had my earlier appeal approved and that unfavorable OER removed from my official file was, I thought, most timely; in May 1971 I was initially considered for temporary promotion to lieutenant colonel (called an AUS promotion). Permanent promotions are based on a specific number of creditable years of service that are set forth in Title 10 of the US Code. There were two Army Promotion Selection Boards that convened to consider eligible officers. The first considered officers of the Army, chaplain, and women's Army Corps. The second (convening about a month later) considered officers of the Dental Corps, Veterinary Corps, Medical Service Corps, Army Nurse Corps, and the Medical Specialist Corps. Some 2,311 officers were being considered for promotion by these boards, and their results would be published concurrently. I was certainly concerned about how my duty performance as a field grade officer would be viewed—especially when compared to others.

No specific criterion exists pertaining to what OER rebuttal information should be submitted. Also, each special review board that evaluates case files is composed of different officers whose assignment is rotated. This means that should you be forced to attack more than one report, information you submit for each action must stand independently and contain all relevant data. When informed that my second rebuttal request was denied, I was told that the information I provided did not justify withdrawing or altering the report in question. This meant that if I still wanted to pursue this action, my case would only be pursued should I submit new, relevant, supplemental data that supported my position. On learning of this disapproval, it prepared me for the information I received later that month. Then I learned that I had not been selected for promotion to lieutenant colonel. Of those officers being considered, I was 1 of 175 that had been selected for retention in grade (not passed over). Because of my earlier successful OER appeal, I was convinced that it was only a matter of time before I would achieve removal of the second report. My file would then be reconsidered for promotion, and I would surely be selected.

On examining the statistical results that came out of this, my sensibilities took a jolt. Of the 2,311 officers that were considered for promotion, 1,332 were selected—a 57.6 percent rate. I was left discouraged because I did not consider myself in the bottom quarter of all majors in the grouping that was studied.

One has to fully evaluate their goals and priorities. Are you willing to devote the necessary hours and live with the many inconveniences *just* to have one bad OER removed from your file? Will that one report really affect your career advancement that much? It is the Army's stated position that "Normally, no single report will serve as the sole basis for any personnel action." Rest assured, one OER can ruin your career. It can certainly prevent you from being promoted or selected for specific assignments. Call it tenacity, call it perseverance, or call it just plain stubbornness—my ire had been raised. Like when I was subjected to pressures in OCS, I was not and am not a quitter. I felt like the gauntlet had been thrown down when my second rebuttal was rejected. The DA's approval of an earlier report followed by the apparent illogical rejection of the second was mind-boggling. I had to pursue it.

Yet, no matter what I seemed to do, the problems didn't seem to stop. I began comparing my difficulties (which certainly weren't as severe) to the torments suffered by Job in the Bible—wondering (as he did), when will they cease? It was now mid-October 1971, time for my annual performance evaluation. Having no trepidations regarding my work and accomplishments, I was truly stunned by my rater's performance evaluation (appendix VIII, page 255, website). Once again, I was damned with faint praise. You will note the use of the word "exceptional" in the rater's narrative, and he scored me numerically with only a 90 percent rating (and to think that's a horrid score?).

As you can tell by my rating officer's narrative, there are no unfavorable comments (referred to as "less than favorable comments" in the Army's vernacular). However, please note the rating in "Part VII, DEMONSTRATED PERFORMANCE OF PRESENT DUTY—PERFORMS THIS DUTY BETTER THAN MOST OFFICERS." Though it sounds good, it is not a helpful rating. Also, being ranked below the TOP group in "Part XII—Overall Value to the Service" will not leave you competitive with other field grade officers when considered for promotion, schooling, or assignments. Even though I believed that this report and the latter report I had received in Korea were detrimental to my career, my conclusions would not be confirmed until after I completed my tour of duty in Hawaii.

Despite everything, I was still determined to eliminate the second OER from my official file. Since nothing is written (for public consumption) regarding what evidence will be considered germane to refute one's OER, I prepared and, on October 12, 1971, submitted the document at appendix IX, page 258 (website), hoping it would be sufficient. At that point, all anyone can do is wait and hope. In early December 1971 I received a second letter. The information I had submitted did not justify altering or removing the report in question from my official file. I was never advised why. So—back to the drawing board.

Though being afforded the privilege of living and working in this island paradise, my experiences with rating officers did little to contribute to my enjoyment of the surroundings. However, I refused to be depressed. I had begun to work in earnest toward completion of my undergraduate degree. I was allowed to complete the requisite hours to receive my baccalaureate degree while continuing to perform my military duties.

Later in December 1971, I (along with many others) walked across the stage at Chaminade College of Honolulu and received that sheepskin (almost fifteen years after entering the Army). Before this, I couldn't even begin to count the number of times my wife said, "Paul, why don't you get out of the Army? You can finish your degree and then go back to active duty!"

For this graduation, my mother and aunt flew in from Houston, Texas, and spent that Christmas season with us. Everyone in the family was bursting with pride. Receiving my undergraduate degree would only help to favorably sway *the promotion bo*ard. My wife was the only family member who knew my problems. How do you explain something that defies the laws of probability? That everyone is out of step but you? Was something truly wrong with me?

I wanted to share the Oahu attractions with my relatives and make them feel just like tourists. So, on December 31, we began a trip around the island (my wife stayed home with our son and daughter). The day was overcast and cool, with periodic showers and a heavy mist. While traveling north on Kamehameha Highway above Punaluu, we observed this Hawaii Visitors and Convention Bureau Warrior's marker on the highway. This marker, coupled with another large white wooden sign, invited visitors to view a natural scenic attraction: Sacred Falls.

Before continuing to the falls, the parking attendant advised us that the trail was slippery. He checked to see that my mother's and aunt's shoes had rubber soles. With his comment, "You shouldn't have any trouble," we started our walk to the falls. We were not informed that the trail had been closed due to rainy weather which created hazardous conditions. Clouds were hanging heavy on the mountain tops and prevented sunshine from filtering into that area.

As we went up the trail (about one-eighth mile), it began to rain. It thoroughly soaked us, and we decided to continue to the falls because we couldn't get any wetter. We were passed by a couple returning from the falls. They told us we would have to cross Kaluanui Stream twice.

When we reached the initial ford, a group of Samoans helped my mother and aunt cross the stream, which was maybe ten feet wide. The water was fairly shallow and barely covered some submerged rocks (which we used as stepping stones). A manila rope strung between trees on opposite sides of the bank paralleled the stepping stones to provide some stability to travelers.

We continued our journey along the southern bank until we reached the second ford, which was too treacherous for my mother and aunt. I helped them to a vantage point. Even from a distance, the cascading beauty dropped several hundred feet and created a showering spray.

Retracing our steps, I got my mother back across the stream. While in the center of the stream, a young boy came running across the ford, shouting, "Help, my father and sister are in the water coming downstream. I've got to get the police." I watched him safely reach the north bank, where my mother was positioned, looked upstream, and saw a *wall* of water coming at me.

When it hit me, I grabbed the manila rope that paralleled the ford. The force of the water and the weight of my body snapped the rope, and I was swept downstream. My body was battered by the rocks. Then I was able to grab some tree branches. This, however, gave me a brief respite. The force of the water ripped off my shoes. All too soon, the surging torrent literally tore me away, and I continued to be swept downstream. I realized that should I strike my head on any rocks, death was imminent. I could finally grasp small tree trunks growing from the south bank. After a hard, exhausting struggle, swallowing a great deal of water, I extricated myself.

I then began to fight my way through some virgin underbrush to let my mother and aunt know I was alive. I remembered their helpless expressions as they watched me being swept away. My trousers were shredded. My Bulova time-zone watch that I had enjoyed for years was ruined. After crossing ridge lines and depressions, I returned to the initial ford. No one was there, and my right eye was bothering me. I was concerned for my aunt's safety.

Soon after I returned to the initial ford, a gray-bearded gentleman, wearing a black leather jacket and a sailor's hat, appeared on the north bank. I asked if he had seen my mother. He had not and advised me to wait for a rescue team. My aunt returned. She had gone to higher ground.

An hour later, a rescue team came, and my aunt and I were able to cross the stream at the initial ford. We walked the distance to find my mother. She was not in the parking lot.

Waiting and watching, we observed other visitors aided by rescue teams as they exited the inundated area. We also observed the removal of two unfortunate drowning victims. These victims were a part of the group who had helped my mother and aunt cross the stream. Finally, the rescue workers brought my mother out. In her efforts to reach the parking area for help, she had climbed to a point where she could not remove herself without assistance.

I was taken to the Kahuku Hospital emergency room for treatment. For the next week, I was required to wear a pressure bandage over my right eye while the corneal abrasion healed. My recovery was followed by an ophthalmologist at Tripler Army Medical Center. Foreign specks were scraped from the cornea and cultured for infection. Fortunately, none was found. A couple of weeks later, a small subepithelial scar and minute foreign bodies were present. These have not created any difficulty. The bruises and lacerations below the waist disappeared.

During our wait for my mother, we talked to the people who operated the parking area. No modern improvement to provide easier visitor access was wanted. Their intent was to retain the rustic conditions as long as possible. From my perspective, a simple bridge could help. This would not detract from the rustic atmosphere or scenic beauty and could have prevented the

1971 New Year's Eve disaster. To invite visitors to hazardous conditions is thoughtless. I expressed my feelings, in writing, to the Bishop Estate Trustees (the owner of this area) in January 1972. Having never returned to this site, I don't know if any changes ever occurred.

My heart went out to the family members whose relatives had perished. They, like me, were only trying to enjoy life. This tragic event received broad media coverage.

Not long after this incident, the lieutenant colonel, for whom I worked, retired from active military service. This occurred less than ninety days after he wrote my annual evaluation, so no report on the performance of my duties since that date was required. His replacement was a breath of fresh air. I did not change the manner in which I accomplished my duties, and his appraisal was even better than some of the reports I received at the Engineer School. When I left Hawaii in the end of July 1972, the rating officer's narrative portion of my OER reflected that I had "... habitually performed all assigned duties in a meticulous, exact and businesslike manner. He is always alert as to where the command emphasis is, and he always ensures that the assets he controls are appropriately oriented. He relentlessly pursues his objectives and never relaxes his efforts until all goals are satisfied. He is a proud, dedicated officer who is determined to attain the high standards he has set for himself. He is a positive thinker, who possesses the ability to orchestrate a myriad of projects at the same time." Likewise, in the indorsing officer's narrative, the colonel stated, [I have] ". . . consistently demonstrated outstanding professional competence in the performance of all duties. He is absolutely trustworthy. When given a mission there is absolutely no worry as to its accomplishment. MAJ [Major] Kirn is a dedicated professional officer and I would fight for his assignment to any organization I might command." During this rating period, I came very close to walking on water.

Reflecting on my rating experiences since I left the Engineer School, I did a lot of soul-searching to understand what happened. I was definitely not pleased with my last report in Korea, nor the annual report as a field artillery adviser to the Hawaii National Guard; yet I hoped that maybe I was being paranoid and my contemporaries were possibly receiving comparable reports. So, I was still faced with the rejection of my attempts to eliminate the second report. Trying again, I submitted my second rebuttal action (appendix X, page 269, website) just before I left Hawaii, feeling confident that rational minds would agree with my position and eliminate this report from my official files.

CHAPTER 8

The Battle Continues

After I completed my tour of duty in paradise, I found myself ordered to duty in purgatory: Fort Polk, Louisiana. I say that in jest. The images conjured up by many who were there during World War II, the Korean conflict, and even the 1950s and 1960s are not pleasant. But things do change. Even prior to my arrival, money had been allocated, and construction was underway to replace and eliminate the many wooden barracks and buildings that had long housed the soldiers serving there. Today, it compares favorably to fine college dormitories. There is a beautiful new commissary, a fine post exchange, a permanent, modern hospital, an attractive post chapel, and many other niceties that contribute to far more pleasant conditions.

When we returned to the mainland, I didn't even consider trying to duplicate the ocean voyage that had taken us to Hawaii. This time we traveled by air. Our daughter was not enamored with the prospects of driving across the country. So we put her on a plane to Houston, where she would stay with her grandmother until we arrived. We had shipped our car to San Francisco when the three of us (wife, son, and I) disembarked after our flight from Hawaii.

Having come to San Francisco three years prior via the southern route, we decided we would explore the Pacific Northwest, go across the northern states, and drop down to

Texas through. The weather was simply gorgeous. Leaving San Francisco, we hugged the California coast on Highway 1. The vistas were breathtaking, including the Redwood National Park in Northern California. Being tourists, we ventured into Oregon and stopped by Crater Lake National Park. Having just come from the region of the world's most active volcanoes, we were anxious to view the topography and compare the two. Moving further north into Washington, we traveled through the Yakima Indian Reservation and over to Spokane. We really enjoyed the mountainous terrain, which was markedly different from Hawaii. After driving across the northern tip of Idaho and into Montana, we appreciated the Rocky Mountain vistas. About halfway through the state, we dropped to Yellowstone National Park, with its friendly bears and Old Faithful. Leaving Yellowstone, we sauntered into the northern reaches of Wyoming and crossed into South Dakota near Rapid City. We viewed the famous Mount Rushmore National Monument and started our trek through the Great Plains (Nebraska, Kansas), Oklahoma, and Texas.

After picking up our daughter in Houston, we continued to Fort Polk, Louisiana, where I would spend the last five years of my active military career. Fort Polk's primary focus was to provide BCT to the Army's new inductees. Always having an opportunity to learn something new, I was assigned duties as the adjutant (brigade S-1) of the 1st BCT Brigade. However, before dedicating myself to these new responsibilities, I had to settle my family in reasonable accommodations. Government housing was virtually nonexistent (a fact that changed tremendously while I was there). For the first time in my life, I bought a home in a subdivision north of DeRidder (twelve miles south of the post). I was confident that my family would be secure, allowing me to concentrate on producing desired results.

Having just completed my undergraduate degree (a major

achievement for me), I finally found myself on a level playing field with the vast majority of commissioned officers. To make myself more competitive, I pursued a master's degree. My experiences with performance ratings would demand that I do something to elevate me above the fray. Regardless of the outcome, I believed that the degree would be of long-term, personal benefit. It was August 1972, and my new position made me responsible for administrative and personnel actions within the brigade. Let me make one thing clear: I was blessed with a tremendous number of capable and dedicated people who worked with and for me. Without them, I would have never been successful.

At this point, you must realize that virtually everyone at your location is aware that you were not selected for promotion to the next higher grade. It's common practice at all military installations for an officer's roster to be published with your duty assignment, rank (or grade), and date of rank. If these are prepared after a promotion list is published, it is also common to place a "P" after one's rank to afford proper recognition to selected officers in a promotable status. Thus, others will begin to wonder how you ruined your career or what has prevented you from being promoted. You will feel like a second-class citizen. Many captains, majors, and lieutenant colonels appear to be much older, over-the-hill types. These officers seem to be relegated to menial tasks, with little visibility, because they are not dynamic thinkers or performers. The capable, outstanding commanders vying for advancement and upward mobility shy away from anyone not promoted. Once again, I was fortunate. Because of my youth, I was not grouped into this crowd. I found myself working for the capable, outstanding commander. He had not come to any preconceived conclusions about my abilities. This brigade commander believed in mission-type orders. You were told what needed to be done and expected to do it. He was not a micromanager, knowing that there are many ways to complete one's assignment. Thus, you were afforded the opportunity to produce desired results and given credit for your work.

To better understand my situation, I was granted a brief leave of absence in September 1972 and went to visit the Field Artillery Branch in Washington, DC, which receives copies of OERs on every officer. They can certainly detect which officers appear to be functioning at a lower than acceptable level. What I feared was a reality. My three OERs reflected ratings below those of my peers. It was suggested that, if possible, I take action to have them modified or removed from my official records. Any uniformed officer would believe that reports comparable to the one I received in Korea and the one as a National Guard adviser would not be damaging. This revelation would have shocked me had I not suspected the circumstances.

Now the fun really begins. Appropriate data (I hoped) had already been submitted to eliminate the May 13, 1970, to Oct 9, 1970, report. To effectively address the shortcomings reflected in the other two reports I had to locate, contact, and solicit the help of third parties. This was becoming a horrendous administrative burden, especially regarding finding the officers who were in Korea with me. Significant time was spent after hours talking with appropriate career branches and individuals. Writing to these people became a necessary part of my life. Remember, these third parties are primarily concerned with their daily activities, and explaining matters over the phone never seemed to convey as much as the written word. Many times, I would send a draft letter of support for their consideration. I would even offer to type any correspondence they might prepare for me should they lack secretarial support. I did whatever I thought would help.

However, before I could begin to effectively collate the appropriate rebuttal data, I had a job. I aggressively studied my responsibilities and sphere of influence. Being aware of one's resources is critical. Know your strengths and weaknesses. I don't believe I approached these tasks differently than before. Yet my rating and indorsing officers gave me full credit for my efforts. I walked on water. They wrote, he "applied himself selflessly to achieve complete mastery over the functions of S-1." Additionally, my rating officer (the brigade executive officer) said I was a "scrupulous, tireless, knowledgeable and dedicated officer who assimilates complex matter rapidly and methodically analyzes all facets in arriving at sound conclusions and recommendations." My rater also mentioned that I should be considered for immediate attendance at the Command and General Staff College. In my indorsing officer's comments, he stated, "He is thoroughly conversant with all regulations and policies and has been totally responsive to the needs of the Brigade. I know of no other officer more capable in the field of personnel. Major Kirn is an outstanding officer who should be selected for promotion to the next higher grade."

This initial OER as brigade adjutant was the last report I received on DA Form 67-6 and was prepared because my rating officer retired. I did nothing to tarnish my image with regard to my new rating officer's perspective. Because I had been selected to perform a special detail, another OER delineating my duty performance had to be prepared. This was one of the first reports on DA Form 67-7 under new guidelines. Thus, the combined scores of my rating and indorsing officers totaled *only* 196 out of 200 so I didn't quite walk on water—but came close.

While establishing myself as the brigade adjutant, before beginning my new duties, I had gathered appropriate information to effect modification of the OER in Korea (appendix XI, page 258, website). This was submitted to the Army Board for Correction of Military Records (ABCMR), reflecting my efforts to finally get this thorn out of my side. It contains my initial appeal of March 20, 1973, along with supplemental actions through April 30, 1974. You will feel my frustrations when you read my arguments in the "Reason for Appeal" that justified this submission and earlier ones on August 16, 1973, and February 5, 1974. The information was not considered sufficient to warrant eliminating or modifying the report, which grates on my nerves.

Coincidentally, on March 20, 1973, my contemporaries who had been selected by the 1971 Promotion Selection Boards were promoted to lieutenant colonel. It can take an extended period to exhaust a promotion list. Had I been promoted, it would have come fifteen years after being commissioned as a second lieutenant.

I was detailed to work for three months as the chief of the Special Inspection Team, in the inspector general's office. I learned the value of prudence. It was easy to find mistakes, failings, and gross irregularities. Yet reporting your findings in a written report must be tempered with a softness that does not crucify the inspected individual or activity. The purpose is to have shortcomings corrected and develop procedures to ensure they don't recur. This will not be accomplished if you castigate responsible parties with your words. Inspections are important and cannot be ignored. People will only do what the commander checks. During this rating period, I had to become intimately familiar with unfamiliar regulations. I found many significant deficiencies in the managerial practices I inspected. It was necessary to aggressively challenge existing procedures to decide whether they were adequate and efficient. In fact, Fort Polk's inspector general mentioned in my OER that I "demonstrated marked ability to detect and seek solutions for potential problem areas normally overlooked or discounted by other inspectors. As a result of his findings and recommendations, the installation commander and staff activity heads have become fully informed of the strengths and weaknesses of activities inspected."

Less than thirty days after I started this detail, I received notification dated May 1, 1973, from the second Army promotion selection board that I was once again not selected for promotion, but this was considered my first "pass over." I received a second letter from the DA. Another board had been convened to consider me for promotion to major in the Regular Army. They did not recommend me. I became a "deferred officer." The possibilities of completing twenty years of active service as an officer were looking bleak.

I don't think a clearer picture could have been painted regarding what was required of me to achieve my objective and be promoted to lieutenant colonel. Somehow, I found time to submit my third supplemental rebuttal, appendix XII, page 310 (website). Not wanting to leave any stone unturned, I forwarded the data I prepared to affect modification of the October 9, 1970, to October 8, 1971, OER as a National Guard adviser, which is attached at appendix XIII, page 318 (website). Despite the rebuttal pursuits, I enjoyed my daily work requirements. The demands and challenges allowed me to achieve job satisfaction. In fact, I'm reminded of an old story relating to reporting for pay. When I entered the Army (the "brown-shoe Army"), soldiers received cash payments at the end of each month. The enlisted personnel would be assembled in alphabetical order, approach the pay officer, snap to attention, and salute while saying, for example, "Sir, Private Kirn reporting for pay." Your pay would then be counted out in front of you, after which you would sign the payroll roster. There were individuals who would goof off and shirk responsibilities. Others would know who these people were and make comments like "Considering how little you've done this month, are you going to back up to the pay table today?" Throughout my career, I never believed I should have backed up to the pay table. Whether in the Army or another job, no employer should have to pay you for less than expected services.

Following my details with the inspector general's office, I returned to work as the adjutant of the 1st BCT brigade. By this time, several senior officers who knew me were becoming chagrined with respect to understanding what I had to do to be selected for promotion to lieutenant colonel. They were pleased with everything I was doing and had no doubt I should be advanced.

Finally, I received a letter from the DA's Evaluation Report Branch dated July 25, 1973, and I was ecstatic (appendix XIV, page 340, website). Two more of my appeals had been approved. Now, almost everything I had worked for had been accomplished. The May 13, 1970, to October 8, 1970, period at KMC had been declared a second nonrated period, withdrawn from my file. Additionally, the rater's portion of my October 9, 1970, to October 8, 1971, efficiency report was deleted (the indorser's numerical ratings were doubled for statistical purposes).

Your attention is invited to the indorsing officer's forwarding remarks in CMT 2 of my May 16, 1971, letter (appendix XII, page 314, website), which undoubtedly showed his personal bias toward me. His request that I be relieved of my responsibilities was denied. I believe this was the key to the approval of my appeal regarding my second KMC report.

Collectively, the many third-party letters of support topped by the December 21, 1972, letter from my rating officer (appendix XIII, page 318, website) specifically portrayed why his evaluation of my duty performance had not been objective. Thus, the appeal of my National Guard rating had been proven and accepted.

My hopes really soared. I firmly believed I had done what was outlined to correct my work record. What could stand in my way? This modification meant that my file would automatically be reviewed by the next board. I would be reconsidered for promotion.

My work performance had not suffered. In fact, between July 2, 1973, and February 2, 1974, I received two OERs prepared under the provisions of paragraph 2-2g, AR 623-105. This said, "When in the opinion of the rater, the rated officer's performance of duty has been so outstanding that a special evaluation report is justified. Distinctly outstanding performance is the absolute prerequisite for such a report."

By coincidence, on July 25, 1973, I happened to call the Field Artillery Branch in Washington, DC. I spoke to Mrs. Anne in the OER appeal's section. She mentioned the recent appeal's approvals. I mentioned that a board to consider officers for promotion to lieutenant colonel was to convene around August. She said she would do all she could to get my records before that board.

On August 2, 1973, I called Ms. Jane in the Officer Promotion Section. She told me that both the Regular Army major and temporary lieutenant colonel standby boards were held on August 1, 1973. My records were not reviewed; they were not able to obtain and prepare them in time. Another standby board would probably not convene for at least another six months.

There have been bureaucratic nightmares associated with trying to achieve results with governmental entities. I should not have expected everything to move with regularity.

On September 14, 1973, I received a postcard from ABCMR advising me that my application (pursuing modification of my December 21, 1968 to June 11, 1969, OER) had been received and would be processed in due time. Knowing they would require my official military file, which was being held by the secretariat for DA Selection Boards to accomplish their adjudicative action, I called ABCMR and told them where it was. I was hoping ABCMR would obtain my file and accomplish the desired action within six months.

Perhaps the only *regularity* one may encounter in the military is change. Checking with ABCMR on October 1, they told me that my official records had been requested from the secretariat for DA Selection Boards but they had not been received. Then, on October 5, I contacted the secretariat for DA Selection Boards to learn when my records had been sent to ABCMR. I was told my official files could not be found and a standby promotion board was to be convened on October 12, 1973.

Certainly, I was concerned. Without my records, I know I couldn't be considered for promotion. I contacted the DA Personnel Records Division, made them aware that my official records were lost, and solicited their assistance in finding my files. All efforts were in vain.

Now, on October 9, I checked again with the secretariat for DA Selection Boards. My official records could not be found, but they would obtain my Field Artillery Branch file, which would suffice for the forthcoming promotion action. Checking again on October 11, my Field Artillery Branch file was in their possession and would be reviewed by October 12.

It was October 15 when I spoke with Major Tom in the Field Artillery Branch. The October 12 board had selected me to be promoted to Regular Army major. Time limitations had precluded the board's consideration of eligible officers for promotion to AUS lieutenant colonel. For me, this was a blessing. Promotion to major in the Regular Army allowed me to complete twenty years of active service and retire with appropriate benefits. The law says that someone on a recommended list or holding the regular grade of major will be retained on active duty until he completes twenty-one years of service. Because of my age, I could remain on active duty for more than twenty-three years, had I elected to do so. Administratively, things move very slowly. My Regular Army promotion required congressional approval, and on January 14, 1974, promotion orders were published, giving me a Regular Army date of rank as a major on July 28, 1973. This date corresponded to fourteen years from the date of my integration into the Regular Army.

I asked Major Tom to have my official military file reconstructed so records would be available for subsequent actions. "We'll take necessary action," they said.

Not wanting to leave anything to chance, on November 6, I called the secretariat. My official military file had not been found. A standby board considering eligible officers for promotion to AUS lieutenant colonel was to be convened the week of November 12. I learned my Field Artillery Branch file was with ABCMR, and nothing had been done to reconstruct my lost official file. They assured me my records would be obtained. On November 8, my records had not been obtained. On November 9, my records had not been obtained by the board scheduled to convene on November 15, 1973. On November 13, my records still had not been obtained. However, Mrs. Mary obtained my reconstructed file (duplicated from my Field Artillery Branch file). She had my file and it would be considered by the November 15 board.

At 3:30 p.m. on November 15, I talked to Mr. Pete. Mrs. Mary gave him my file, and he found it was not properly constituted. Mr. Pete was not able to prepare my file for presentation to the board until 2 p.m., November 15 (after the AUS lieutenant colonel board had adjourned).

Following this experience, I called Lieutenant Colonel Jack, DA Standby Promotion Board Recorder, and outlined the above circumstances, which could be described as "almost criminal," and would sorely try the patience of Job. She discussed the matter with her superior and was directed to reconstitute another standby AUS lieutenant colonel's board to convene at the earliest practicable date. This board was convened on November 19, and my file was reconsidered under the criteria of the 1971 and 1972 boards. Once again, my efforts accomplished nothing. This board also failed to consider me for promotion to lieutenant colonel.

So, where do I go from here?

CHAPTER 9

Promotion Achieved

I still had my pride. Also, my determination was intact. Others were not aware that these repeated rejections were aggravating. I was not going to give up. I struggled, racking my brain trying to conjure up that piece of evidence that would prove my case. From the outside, they see an officer who worked almost three years under four different rating officers. This officer has apparently been of questionable value to the Army. Since probably no other officer has ever successfully rebutted three successive evaluations, members of promotion boards are befuddled when they view my file. Historically, they know that no one has to challenge more than one OER. After all, the established safeguards preclude the necessity of anyone having to rebut a performance evaluation. Maybe one report could have slipped through, but how could anyone have to challenge *four*? It was easier for those reviewing my case to decide, "He's not qualified."

I'm not so naive that I believe I'm the only officer in the Army's history who has performed in a noteworthy manner and didn't receive rightful credit. Many have experienced similar conditions and left without fulfillment and with bitter feelings. However, it's obvious that I come from a *different* mold. Whether it's genetics or fate, all my inner forces were mobilized to attack this problem, something I was going to do until I achieved some type of closure.

Once again, I turned to my court of last resort—ABCMR

(appendix XI page 279, website), TAB B REASON FOR APPEAL, dated February 5, 1974. Maybe I subconsciously believed in the Chinese water torture theory. *Eventually they're going to get too frustrated and surrender*, I thought.

I worked as the 1st BCT Brigade adjutant until early May 1974. At this time, Fort Polk's basic training functions were being phased out, and preparations to house the 5th Infantry Division were receiving more emphasis. In my last evaluation as an adjutant, my rating officer reflected the following: "During the rated period, it was not possible for Major Kirn to perform in a more outstanding manner. Under his auspices, administrative guidance concerning the proper submission of many types of discharge actions was prepared and appropriately updated which positively resolved questions that might otherwise have arisen. This action allowed the expeditious flow of correspondence to occur within this command. Extremely noteworthy has been this officer's ability to write in a manner which dynamically conveys the desired message—a talent infrequently encountered these days. It has truly been a pleasure to observe Major Kirn confidently and expertly complete or supervise/direct the completion of all tasks associated with his sphere of influence. To further develop his abilities and improve his military prowess, this officer has enrolled in the nonresident Command and General Staff Officer Course. This officer is certainly worthy of immediate promotion to Lieutenant Colonel." This summary was endorsed by the brigade commander, who stated, "Major Kirn has indeed performed his duties in an outstanding manner. He is extremely conscientious, dedicated and completely professional. He has superb ability to anticipate needs and requirements and as a result is 'on top of the situation' before it develops. Major Kirn has demonstrated a keen organizational ability and an uncommonly high degree of initiative. In addition to being enrolled in the nonresident CGSO course, he is active in off-duty college programs to acquire a master's degree. Major Kirn and his wife are active in social and community affairs. This officer should be promoted immediately."

My next duty assignment was as chief, Human Relations Division, a general staff position. I served in this position from May 1974 until January 1977. In this position, I was responsible for a program that was receiving more command emphasis beginning at the DA level. I became known as the Installation Alcohol and Drug Control Officer. Organizationally, my division consisted of an Alcohol Rehabilitation Branch, a Professional Services Branch, and an Army Community Services Branch. It was necessary to guide the efforts of counselors, psychiatrists, psychologists, social workers, chaplains, and assigned military personnel while directing an education program designed to resolve difficulties and problems.

Though I had not worked in this field prior to this assignment, I had no reservations regarding my ability. I had certainly not been remiss in pursuing the modification of my official file, and from my perspective, things looked pretty good. Three reports had been successfully challenged, and the information I submitted to challenge the report written in Korea (which remained in my file) would, I thought, be an effective buffer. At this time, my efficiency file reflecting my job performance as a major portrayed (I believed) very creditable service. The numerical scores from these reports are shown in the chart below. The maximum score that one rating official could award on DA Form 67-5 was 120, and on forms DA 67-6 and 67-7, it was 100. I anxiously awaited the results of yet another regularly scheduled promotion selection board that was in session at this time.

Unfortunately, my problem with job performance evaluations had yet to end. In appendix XV, page 342 (website), there are copies of the first couple of OERs I received as chief,

Human Relations Division. As you will see, these contain *glowing* reflections. Believe me, this text is not intended to be self-serving or glorify my accomplishments. It is only through my complete disclosure that you will be able to make an informed decision. (I have purposely eliminated individual names. I have no desire to be vindictive or cause embarrassment.)

Scores Received on OERs as a Major

DA Form	Period	Rater	Endorser
67-5	23 Nov 66—20 Jun 67	117.6	117.8
67-5	21 Jun 67—21 Dec 67	117.0	117.0
67-6	22 Dec 67—5 Apr 68	96	95
67-6	6 Apr 68—20 Dec 68	95	95
67-6	21 Dec 68—11 Jun 69	90	96
	12 Jun 69—12 May 70	*	*
	13 May 70—8 Oct 70	*	*
67-6	9 Oct 70—8 Oct 71	*	95
67-6	9 Oct 71—26 Jul 72	99	96
67-6	27 Jul 72—24 Dec 72	100	100
67-7	25 Dec 72—1 Apr 73	98	98
67-7	2 Apr 73—1 Jul 73	96	96
67-7	2 Jul 73—30 Sep 73	100	98
67-7	1 Nov 73- 25 Feb 74	100	100
67-7	26 Feb 74—27 May 74	100	100

* Nonrated periods (successful rebuttal actions)

With great expectations, I awaited the results of the latest lieutenant colonel's promotion selection board, which was published in July 1974. Imagine my consternation when I was not selected and had now been passed over twice. By this time, I made my presence known, and my new group of officers could hardly believe that I had once again drawn the short straw. I was very thankful that I had persevered and been integrated into the

Regular Army. Had I remained a USAR officer, this second pass over would have required separation from active military service.

Attempting to correct an injustice, my fellow superior officers tried to decide what they could do to change things. The first report, referenced in appendix XV (page 342, website), covered from May 28, 1974, to August 16, 1974, is another special report that demanded walk-on-water ratings or evaluations.

Let me call your attention to a specific change in the new DA Form 67-7, intended to provide critical information to rating officials throughout the Army and hold down numerical scores (reduce inflation). To provide a "measuring stick" allowing Army-wide comparisons, an "average score" for officers in the grade of captain, major, lieutenant colonel, and colonel was published and added to part V and VI for the awareness of rating and indorsing officers. Initially, the average score for a major was 123. Later, all elements of the Army were given a "Mean Score" to use as a gauge: 175 for a major. I compared this data to my evaluations. The lowest score I received as a field grade officer (except the latter Korean report) was 190 (out of 200). This report spanned my initial period of Korean duty from April to December 1968. How does one determine what is actually preventing a promotion? "What more can I do?" I often asked.

Retaining optimism, I believed my efforts seeking modification of the December 1968 to June 1969 OER would be successful. Thus, on October 21, 1974, I submitted yet another appeal to ABCMR (appendix XVI, page 349, website) after receiving their notification that, once again, the information was insufficient. Even with this pending, I tried another approach. Instead of only pursuing modification of the OER I had received in Korea, I filed another appeal with ABCMR, seeking promotion to lieutenant colonel because of the injustices I had experienced. (Appendix XVI, page 349, website: Letters attached at tabs J, K, L, and M have not been duplicated but are included in earlier respective rebuttal data. I also did not duplicate my college transcript at tab N.)

There were several senior officers at Fort Polk aware of my situation—but this was not something I talked about. I was not the only officer who failed to be selected for promotion. Thus, following the publication of the latest lieutenant colonel's results, one of these senior officers asked that a major who worked in a general staff position contact me. This major was an armor officer who, like myself, had been passed over for promotion by the recent board. Aware of my efforts, he hoped I might shed some light on his history and possibly help him achieve his promotion goal. Baring your soul to a stranger is not easy. Fortunately, he had visited the DA and had copies of all his OERs. It was a recent policy change that a copy of the OER was given to the rated officer after preparation. Earlier in my career, you or someone you deputized had to visit the DA to obtain copies of your records. So, going over his total work file, I found no reports that included derogatory information or less than favorable comments. Mentally, I compared his reports to mine. The numerical ratings were much lower, and I didn't believe I could help him. He was certainly a fine officer, but apparently he had been rated lower than his contemporaries. He also hadn't been selected to attend Command and General Staff College. Then, I asked him about a report in Vietnam that spanned less than the ninety-day minimum requirement for evaluation of a field grade officer. It was not a special report, but it reflected 189 or 190 numerical scores from each rating official. At the time this report was prepared, he was being reassigned and his rating officer wanted him to get credit for his work in a combat zone. Candidly, I told him he shouldn't have difficulty getting his report eliminated from his file because it clearly violated the time requirements. Removing it would modify his OMPF, resulting in reconsideration for promotion by the next selection board. Then hope for the best.

This report was successfully challenged, and this major's file was referred to the next standby promotion selection board. This board considered him fully qualified, and he was selected for promotion to lieutenant colonel. I was pleased that I could help someone, and he couldn't have been happier. Challenging this report was not a major administrative task. It required only a letter asking for removal because it violated the regulation.

Just before he retired, the director of community activities who endorsed my last two efficiency reports (appendix XVII, page 371, website) wrote to the deputy chief of staff for personnel (he was about to be promoted to lieutenant general). This letter and response triggered the correspondence at appendix XVII, page 371 (website). You will appreciate my dogged determination with respect to the repeated rejections. And you will learn how I finally achieved my objective.

However, I'm getting ahead of myself. Shortly after the new director of community activities (DCA) was assigned, a personnel realignment occurred to satisfy needs associated with the 5th Infantry Division. This included converting the deputy DCA position to be staffed by a civil service employee. Now, the DCA became my rating officer, and the deputy installation commander was designated as my indorsing officer.

Because I have not named any of my rating officials, I must point out that the deputy installation commander was formerly the chief of staff that reviewed my August 14 to December 22, 1974, OER (appendix XV, page 342, website). For some unknown reason, this colonel was compelled to split hairs: "I feel the perfect score is inflated and 198 is more truly representative of this officer's ability." I never approached this officer to try and learn what shortcomings he believed I possessed but hoped my job performance would overcome his reservations. He was not a warm, congenial individual from whom you could solicit guidance or obtain perspective. This officer wasn't concerned with helping you solve problems; all he wanted was for you to overcome difficulties on your own, or you would be taken to task for failing to do your job. Thus, when I learned that the new DCA (my new rating officer) was not the professional soldier of the caliber one would expect to find as a colonel, I didn't believe my perceptions could be discussed with my indorsing officer. I knew my responsibilities and did everything possible to work around any stumbling blocks.

I was able to recognize patterns. When briefing Colonel Alex in December 1974 on his assignment as DCA, his only question concerning the operation of the Human Relations Division (HRD) was what directive required the submission of the monthly synopsis that I forwarded to the commander. I told him, "Nothing required its submission. However, my total operation was a command program, and I believed the commander should be aware of what went on in this area." Colonel Alex directed that future reports were to be sent only to him. Should he think something in them concerned the command group, he would forward it.

In early January 1975, the report was prepared as previously done (through DCA, chief of staff to commander) and was then forwarded by the DCA staff. When it came back, it contained very favorable comments. These were from the chief of staff (who had not yet become the deputy installation commander) and the commanding general. Strangely, the only comment from the DCA (my boss) was a terse note telling me to "Look at last month's report. Didn't I tell you to keep this in-house?" Receiving this, I quickly went to Colonel Alex's office and apologized for misaddressing the monthly synopsis—it was an oversight. I asked, since such favorable comments had been received from both the chief of staff and commander, if subsequent reports couldn't continue to be forwarded to the command group, and he agreed that this could happen.

While working for this DCA, there was no pleasurable meeting with him. I was always courteous and respectful and treated him with the dignity appropriate for someone of his rank and position. Yet, almost every time I entered his office, he would be ensconced in his chair (wearing cowboy boots with his Class A uniform), and his feet would be propped up on his desk. I would greet him with a salute, and he seemed to be reading a newspaper or magazine. His manner with me was habitually curt, creating a very unpleasant environment.

At this time, I was fighting to excel and receive a valid evaluation of my service. A detailed portrayal of conditions I experienced is described in appendix XIX, page 411 (website), which I will not duplicate here. Because one aspect of the alcohol and drug control program required changing local directives to include Fort Polk's civilian workforce, my proposals required command approval. On January 14, 1975, I attempted to circulate appropriate information. That same day, the deputy DCA called and told me the DCA wouldn't forward it. On January 15, I went to the DCA to clarify any misunderstanding. I was told by the DCA, in the presence of his deputy, that Fort Polk Regulation 600-85 was fine the way it was written and didn't need any change. He also said he was not going to tell civilians what to do, stating that regulations (drug and alcohol) were made for "the guys in the green suits." He would not ask the commanding general what his latitude was—showing he paid little attention to the contents of the document.

Fully believing that the DCA did not understand what I was trying to accomplish, on January 16, I revised my approach with another written effort that was rebuffed. So on January 17, I talked to the DCA in the presence of his deputy. I told him I believed a communication problem existed, and I wasn't trying to "butt heads" with him. He told me if I was, there would only be one loser—me! "I make no bones about it, and I'm very inflexible. Once I make up my mind about something, that's the way it's going to be. If you can't stand the heat, get out of the kitchen," he said. This really discouraged communication. I then called the Field Artillery Branch in Washington, DC. Having then been at Fort Polk for 2.5 years, I asked if they would relocate me to preclude my serving under this DCA for ninety duty days. They refused. Well, I've always been proud of my responsibilities and concern for my people. I had a responsibility to the installation commander and believed I could do an outstanding job, as evidenced by the OERs at appendix XV, page 342 (website). Thus, I discussed conditions candidly with other senior officers at Fort Polk. They suggested I had the ability to work around this DCA, and I should continue to do what I had done in the past. I then resolved to do the best job possible.

My irritation grew on May 21, 1975, when the DCA called a meeting of all subordinate heads. It was attended by myself, the recreation services officer (a lieutenant colonel), and the installation club systems officer (a major). The DCA opened the meeting with the comment that the three of us were about to be relieved. He cited specific areas of dissatisfaction in each section. I was told the chief of staff (soon-to-be endorser on my OER) told him the operation of HRD was unsatisfactory. However, when asked about specifics, the only area mentioned was Army Community Services. He told me I was not properly supervising my division, and if I didn't pump new life into it, I would be relieved. These allegations were rebutted, and the DCA said he thought I was doing a fine job, so just continue to do what I had been doing. After this talk, I asked the DCA if I could talk to the chief of staff, which I attempted to do. Yet when I approached the secretary general staff (a major) for an appointment, I was told that the chief of staff said I didn't need to talk to him; I needed to talk to the DCA.

You've probably read appendix XVII, page 371 (website), and have an appreciation of the exchanges that were occurring. Remember, I was pursuing courses for my master's program and the Command and General Staff Officers Course. Certainly, it relieved some anxieties to learn (August 1975) that my file would be considered by another promotion selection board.

Feeling comfortable that (finally) there was nothing in my OMPF that could negatively influence their decision, I was horrified when I read the new OER from the DCA at appendix XVIII, page 408 (website), which covered my job performance through September 30, 1975. I felt like I'd been *stabbed* in the back. I had already received two walk-on-water performance evaluations. Now, performing the same job, I received a report with adverse comments and a much lower numerical score. This would raise a question in any board member's mind. I understand, when my file is prepared for scrutiny by the board, that this report should not be available for review, as my records were being evaluated for specific earlier periods. Yet, considering what previously happened to my records, I was skeptical regarding what should and would transpire.

Having seen a copy of this OER before it was submitted to the DA, I discussed its contents with the former chief of staff, now the deputy installation commander (DIC)—my indorsing officer. When asked why he refused to see me, he told me he had never refused to see anyone. Later, I spoke with the major, secretary general staff, who confirmed that my request had been refused. The major added that a couple of days after this refusal, I had called him back to tell him I had resolved the matter. I don't recall or believe this. I asked the DIC to identify the superiors and subordinates with whom I had trouble maintaining good communications. He then named the former commanding general's wife, the former deputy commanding general's wife, the colonel's wife, and some sergeant who used to work for me whose name he couldn't remember. The names on his list surprised me, and I told the DIC that I did not consider the people mentioned to be my superiors. We also had a lengthy discussion regarding the miserable conditions I had experienced (which were documented) working under the DCA. Following this discussion, the DIC added the last two sentences to his narrative in part VIIb of the OER at appendix XVIII (page 408, website) and raised his numerical scores in part V and VI one point each. I asked him to hold this OER until the commanding general returned for his review. He refused. He said he considered it inappropriate to have only one report reviewed by a major general and the others prepared by the DCA on his departure reviewed by a brigadier general. The DIC said should I discuss this OER with either of these general officers, it would not influence his rating in any way. I knew that the reviewing officer could attach a clarifying statement to the OER; however, at this time, I concluded that nothing could be gained other than more adverse working relations.

No one ever advised me that I was performing at a level requiring criticism or that I was doing work short of the caliber reflected in the OERs at appendix XV (page 342, website). Maybe I should have reacted differently or been more vocal regarding my working conditions. I'm reminded of an old Indian proverb: "Don't judge a man until you have walked two moons in his moccasins," which is very apropos. My years of service since 1970 had been very trying, and though I never worked for my evaluation, I don't believe I deserved some of the appraisals I received. Possibly had I not experienced similar conditions or been doing my utmost to satisfy my rating officer, I might have been more vocal. Good or bad, we live with our decisions.

Shortly after experiencing the many frustrations dealing with what I believed to be another unfair evaluation, in early October 1975, I learned the standby board selected me for promotion to lieutenant colonel. A copy of this confirmation document, which was finally prepared in November 1975, is the last item attached at appendix XVII (page 371, website). *What a relief!* The board did not consider me qualified for promotion under the criteria established when originally considered in 1971 or again in 1972. They did select me under the criteria of the May 1974 board, and I received a June 2, 1974, date of rank.

Promotion to LTC

Because congressional approval is required, my actual promotion didn't occur until December 19, 1975. I was called into the commanding general's office at Fort Polk and received my silver oak leaves. After the ceremony, the chief of staff who had previously been a brigade commander, under whom I had proudly served as his adjutant, made the following comment: "Paul. You finally made the system work!"

CHAPTER 10

Perspective

I finally reached a form of closure that would allow me to live with myself. However, I cannot say that I am comfortable with the decisions regarding my appeals to ABCMR of the report I received in Korea (appendix XI, page 275, XVI, page 349, and XIX, page 411, website). There is a certain military mindset that exists. People who reach positions of authority believe in the system that allowed them to achieve that status. Thus, there is a reluctance to believe that any condition would warrant a change in the status quo.

It's possible that the conditions relating to OERs that I've discussed herein will forever be a part of the military environment. To create the optimum system that would ensure all officers receive an objective evaluation of their job performance would be a monumental achievement. I would not suggest that I could develop this optimum system. The Army's officer evaluation system is not perfect. The system looks good on paper. However, it is not possible to finitely control the actions of all who must implement the system. Some discrepancies have been highlighted throughout this text. The inequality of the system has been acknowledged by senior officials at all levels. Even the regulation covering preparation of OERs allows for addressing the inequities that the Army knows will occur. Reflecting on the past, I know the ultimate goal of the *perfect rating system* was not achieved and probably has not been attained to this day. However, it's possible that the powers-that-be may not want a perfect rating system. Should perfection exist, possibly a far greater number of men and women would opt to make the Army their career. This would result in only the best qualified personnel receiving promotions. Supposedly, this is what now occurs. However, my experience raises that specter of doubt. With the ideal working atmosphere, fewer people would elect to leave active service, and promotion opportunities would be slower. As patience is not habitually associated with Americans, a greater number of quality officers may elect to leave active military service rather than wait for opportunities. Even though the superior caliber of officers on active duty may increase, the percentage of officers promoted will not necessarily be any greater—because they will be limited by requirements and vacancies. Superficially changing the officer evaluation system every few years may only be a psychological ploy aimed at the multitudes. The military services readily accept the reality that no one is indispensable. Many years ago, it could have been decided that the available labor pool is more than sufficient to supply our country's officer needs. Thus, to modify or create a system that would retain more officers may not be desirable.

You might find yourself working for someone who will not evaluate your services objectively. Thus, you might not satisfy your career objectives. Those around you may express remorse, and you may even be told to pursue the path that I've just exposed. You will have to decide what is best for you. If appealing your evaluation is your only option, is it worth the effort?

When you consider employment possibilities throughout society, it would appear that working in a 200-plus-year-old organization would give you peace of mind and offer job security. What could provide more stability than an organization that has endured the ravages of time and is making changes to adapt?

In fact, all the benefits associated with a military career are set forth in writing—how many employers spell out your benefits and safeguards in an unambiguous manner? Though all of your benefits associated with a military career are published, don't assume that these matters are set in stone. All activities associated with this nation's military are controlled by our government. As such, today's contracts can be subjected to the political whims of our politicians. There are *no guarantees!*

The manner in which an individual's job performance is recorded by others can markedly affect one's military career—determining your ability to retire from active military service after twenty years and receive retirement benefits. The same options that were available to me are not available now. One recent change mandated by Congress is the standardization of regular commissions in all military services. Previously, regular commissions were awarded to graduates of the military academies and top graduates of ROTC programs and officer training schools. Now, all officers entering the services will receive Reserve commissions. Regular commissions will be granted (not something done automatically) only if and when one is promoted to the pay grade O-4 (major/lieutenant commander). This change now allows officers with regular commissions to remain in the active service for up to twenty-eight years. Officers with Reserve commissions must retire at twenty years of service (should their records allow them to reach that plateau). Had this change been implemented prior to the receipt of my regular commission, I might have never achieved or been in a position to pursue the injustice.

An exception to the timetable would be medical officers. Because of schooling, delayed entry factors, experience, etc., some medical officers are commissioned as O-3 or O-4 (captain/major). These individuals must wait until they become O-5s (lieutenant colonel/commander) before they can receive a Regular Army commission.

Knowing the value of an OER, it was always a wonderment that no formal instruction regarding its preparation existed during my period of active duty. My first experience in evaluating the performance of a subordinate was that of my platoon sergeant when I was a second lieutenant. Our personnel officer sent me the necessary forms to complete for an annual evaluation. My platoon sergeant was a dynamic, knowledgeable leader of men and an excellent teacher. I rated his performance objectively, not knowing that the enlisted evaluation system is as inflated as for the officers. How many outstanding enlisted men's careers have been hurt because they received less than competitive evaluations, prepared by naive, uninformed, but well-meaning officers?

An officer can experience a similar situation. Certainly, the regulation that directs the preparation of an OER requires that a report reflect total accuracy and objectivity. The veracity of any officer who would *swear* that every report he or she prepared (as a rater, indorser, or reviewer) was not in any way subjective is questionable. Human traits automatically compare the talents and abilities of one individual to another—subjectively. You may deny it, and I have no doubt you can support your position should it be challenged. The facts associated with this area are rife with perceptions and semantics. Suppose your rating officer believes in meeting after work at the Officer's Club for a social drink to discuss the day's activities. The other four officers who work for him are drinking various alcoholic beverages while you are consuming a coke. This may and should have no bearing on your evaluation, but the Army is composed of human beings. Can I know that some of my evaluations were not adversely affected by the fact that I don't drink alcohol or smoke cigarettes? Would I be viewed differently (to my detriment)?

Consider that you're working for an officer who is being forced to retire at a certain rank when that person believes they should have been promoted. Bitterness is harbored by this officer regarding a military career. Are evaluations going to be objective? Maybe this officer believes the evaluations are adequate. Can you be sure they are objective?

I wish I possessed the infinite wisdom to help foster the development of the perfect evaluation method. If everyone would follow the existing regulation, the system would be adequate. But no two officers will express themselves identically. What one officer may view as a superior effort might be outstanding or subpar to another. Who determines which adjective best describes a condition? Is the rating officer swayed by some meaningless situation? About midway through my career, I was given an information sheet on grammar, (appendix XXI, page 467, website). This document might be beneficial to you.

To help you understand how competitive advancement is in the military, let me share some figures taken from Title 10 of the US Code in the chart below. The initial figure reflects the number of commissioned officers (with some exceptions) on active duty by service. This is then followed by the number of officers authorized to serve on active duty at that force level in the grade of major, lieutenant colonel, and colonel. (Navy designation is lieutenant commander, commander, and captain.)

	OFFICER LEVEL	MAJOR	LIEUTENANT COLONEL	COLONEL
Army:	170,000	26,793	16,488	7,116
Air Force:	125,000	21,626	13,539	5,378
Marine Corps:	25,000	4,042	1,865	695
Navy:	90,000	15,739	8,886	4,013

The above figures are just portions of the staffing table in Title 10. Predetermined force levels have been established by members of Congress to meet varying levels of commitment throughout the world. Statistically, it's easy to see that everyone who reaches one career plateau will not make it to the next level.

It would be fallacious to suggest or infer that all military officers will be exposed to conditions similar to mine. Fortunately, the majority of military officers are not confronted with these experiences. Unfortunately, historical data shows that this type of unwanted circumstance has occurred, and the future is likely to behave like the past. No matter how small the number of officers who are faced with unfair or inaccurate performance evaluations, one is too many—especially if you are that one!

Do you believe your OMPF contains an evaluation report or reports that can adversely affect your career? If so, I would suggest that you pointedly ask your career branch what course of action they recommend. Should you be told that one (or more) report(s) is detrimental, decide if continuing active duty in the military is best for you. Appealing an OER is an individual determination. Each person must decide if a report accurately or objectively reflects the manner in which they performed their duties. Then, can you prove that an evaluation is invalid? Is it worth the effort? Will there be consequences? Is this what you want or have to do? Knowing that each officer must rely on their intelligence, intuitive nature, and knowledge of circumstances, attaining modification or elimination of an OER will not be an easy task. Pursuit of your goal is made doubly hard because you are not privy to the instructions given to special review board members who review your appeal. You do not know what parameters are used to gauge the information you submit.

Weighing these factors, about nine months after I was promoted, I filed the appeal at appendix XIX, page 411 (website). Once again, I had drawn the short straw with regard to my rating officer. I took this action because I did not want the information to remain unchallenged in my OMPF. Believe me, I had no illusions about my future advancement. I knew that the guiding regulation prohibits any rater who is relieved of his duties for cause from rating officers formerly under his command or supervision. Having heard that my rating officer was relieved for cause, I believed it would be easier to attack his evaluation of my services than risk being rated by my indorsing officer (the alternative mandated by regulation). Several questions may arise as you read this appeal and attempt to correlate the DA's December 3, 1996, response at the end of appendix XIX (page 457, website) to the information I submitted. One major point that this response does not address is the contested accuracy or disputed objectivity of the report. I believed the information I provided would prove that my rating officer was relieved for cause. Additionally, the letter attached as tab A to appendix XIX (page 418, website) and the supporting information would more than establish that my evaluation was not objective. Thus, I did not go to greater lengths to obtain additional supporting documents. When my appeal was rejected, I could have attempted to obtain confirmation from the colonel's branch in Washington, DC, regarding what they were told to obtain funding for the relocation expenses of my rating officer. Apparently, senior officers failed to do what was proper, and this colonel, who was not relieved for cause, was allowed to go elsewhere and further damage the Army's image and possibly the careers of other officers. At this time, I didn't believe that further pursuit of this appeal was worth my time or effort.

Fully realizing that events were not going to affect the remainder of my active military career, I was truly astounded by the contents of a package delivered by USPS in late 1976. A branch of the University of Wisconsin sent me the vast majority of my "lost" OMPF (all but the OER section). The unsigned and undated transmittal note on their letter head read as follows:

INSTITUTE FOR RESEARCH ON POVERTY
THE UNIVERSITY OF WISCONSIN
262-6358 AREA CODE 608

SOCIAL SCIENCE BUILDING
1180 OBSERVATORY DRIVE
MADISON, WISCONSIN 53706

Dear Sirs

The enclosed materials have been mistakenly sent to us. We are sending them to you in hopes that either you are the proper recipient or that you will be able to get these materials to the proper recipient.

Thank you

I did not believe anything could be gained by sending these files back to the DA, so I just kept them. How and why they arrived at the Institute for Research on Poverty boggles my mind.

Thankful and glad that I had finally been promoted, I submitted the letters at appendix XX (page 458, website), hoping to trigger additional favorable action. This did not occur.

Regarding my promotion to lieutenant colonel, here are some major points.

- I did receive the pay differential between that of a major and a lieutenant colonel back to the date of my promotion (June 2, 1974). Existing regulations allow for this. I also asked for interest on the money withheld (like you will be charged by the IRS on any late payments), which was denied. It could have been obtained if I requested my congressman introduce a separate pay bill for that amount.

- Had experiences, schooling, and assignments been different, I could have gone further with my military career.
- Many officers have experienced miserable working conditions during their tours of active duty. Active military services have failed to retain some exceptionally talented officers because of unacceptable working conditions.
- Having decided that continuing my military career well beyond the twenty-year mark was not going to happen, I let my enrollment in the Command and General Staff College lapse.
- In May 1977, I was awarded my master of arts degree from Central Michigan University.
- I finally came to a conclusion regarding the OER I received in Korea, which I repeatedly/unsuccessfully appealed (Dec 21, 1968, to June 11, 1969). After receiving notice of my pending promotion, I spoke with the officer at the DA who had followed my appeal actions. He shared, "Paul, you'll never get that OER modified based on what you've submitted." I was taken aback. Reviewing my data, I believe the March 2, 1973, letter from my indorsing officer (Incl. 3 Tab D, appendix XI, page 285, website) stated that he discussed my evaluation with my rating officer before it was submitted. It says, "I discussed this with the Rating Officer, who however, chose not to change his rating." The rating officer concluded that his rating was objective. Thus, future statements from the rating officer were meaningless. Had this statement not been a part of my effort, I believe my appeal had sufficient third-party statements to allow a favorable conclusion. There are *no* guarantees.

My intent is to provide information that will help you in your career decisions. We would all like to be happy in whatever we do. In this regard, several years ago, I wrote the following:

HAPPINESS

The quest for happiness is a universal thrust. Some make it their primary objective, yet others find it a byproduct of their efforts. Locating this euphoric feeling, for many individuals, is as elusive as "finding that pot of gold at the end of the rainbow." However, those who can wrap themselves in its aura can experience an incomparable feeling of ecstasy. Retention of this ecstatic feeling throughout one's life is certainly a desirable end. There are those who, during their lifetime, walk in the highways and byways of life, always searching for and never finding or experiencing happiness. For others, it can be a fleeting event, while some enjoy its delights for extended periods. Whenever or however it is experienced, it is truly a memorable moment.

Each person will know when happiness is found, and unique experiences will selectively determine what sensibilities will be appropriately aroused. Normally, happiness is created through a shared experience—a total giving, one to the other. This feeling can be enhanced by nice tidbits, such as candles in a darkened room, a moonlit ride on a ferryboat, or simply being together—alone. Whatever creates an individual's happiness is unimportant when compared to the lifelong memory—being able to relive that time forever and ever.

It would be wonderful if happiness, once found, could be maintained, preserved for posterity. Then, one truly could find heaven on Earth. Seeking happiness is certainly worth the effort because finding it is like locating the greatest treasure known to mankind. Once found, one will strive to hold onto it. If it is true happiness, that person would never do anything to alter that condition or damage that cherished memory. Knowing happiness in one's lifetime is truly a wonderful experience—worth striving to find and taking risks to enjoy.

> All of one's life is a challenge. And everyone must work for their successes.

Now, upon reflection, there is another verse I found that belonged to my father. This coincided with the educational function of my duties as ADCO while in the service. Had I known of its existence at that time, it may have appropriately piqued someone's interest just enough to save a life. Although I do not know the original author, Ann Landers mentioned it in *The Palladium-Times* on page eight, published February 23, 1993.

RECIPE FOR A POPULAR FUNERAL
Take one natural born fool,
Two drinks of beer or whiskey,
Mix in a high-powered automobile.
When the fool is well soaked,
Place his foot on the gas, release brakes.
Remove the fool from the wreck,
Gather up the killed and wounded,
Place the fool in a silk-lined box,
Garnish with flowers and money,
Use a popular preacher.
Thousands will attend.

It is my hope that, with the information I've provided, you will be in a much better position to evaluate your career aspirations. Many may believe that I violated the *DARN* principle from chapter 1. In my defense, without *discipline*, this book could not have been written. My goal was *achieved*. The *result* is that it is published. The *now* aspect would lead one to believe I procrastinated for many years. My perspective has certainly changed and matured since retirement. The time delay has allowed me to portray a valid historical perspective of my career. An earlier attempt might have contained inappropriate feelings that detracted from its purpose. You have been given the facts; it's now time for you to draw your own conclusions.

Reflecting on my decisions, would I pursue a career in the Army again? *Yes!* I did not come from a family of great wealth, where infinite possibilities (education and employment) were available. Should I do it again, I would hope that my job evaluation experiences would not recur, although undesirable or unexpected situations probably still occur today. Programs allow military members to do nothing but attend institutes of higher learning and receive degrees at all levels (appendix XXII, page 472, website). Though I was not selected for one of these programs, I did complete my undergraduate and master's programs before I retired. Entering the Army as a private (E-1), I was afforded opportunities and retired as a lieutenant colonel (O-5). My career provided job satisfaction, growth, travel, and experiences that could not have been duplicated in another career path. This profession allowed me to provide for my family, which was always important to me. The medical and dental benefits are invaluable perks. My appreciation for this country and our ancestors' sacrifices makes me a proud American. So, on October 1, 1977, at thirty-nine years of age, I retired and was credited with twenty-one years of active military service.

No matter what your career choice, the most important attribute you can display is your *attitude*. If it's pleasant, people will always be willing to help you. Don't wait for something to happen—make it happen. As an adult, no one owes you anything. You have to earn what you get. Pick yourself up and stand on your own two feet. If things don't go as planned, do something different. You may have to fight for your convictions—have courage. Ensure your convictions are well-founded. Be reasonable and listen to other viewpoints. Don't be inflexible.

To the people who worked with me and for me throughout my career, your contributions, accomplishments, and teamwork were invaluable. It is not possible to sufficiently express my gratitude to the individuals who helped me succeed in my rebuttal actions and promotion. Though I personally tried to prepare much of the correspondence relating to my appeals, the secretarial support I enjoyed during my later years at Fort Polk was truly priceless. My sincere thanks to all.

Should you believe filing an OER appeal is appropriate, I suggest you look at my guidance in appendix XXIII, page 474, available at https://retltcpaulkirn.wordpress.com/.

GOOD LUCK.

ABOUT THE AUTHOR

Paul L. Kirn was born in San Antonio, Texas. He moved to Houston as an infant and remained there until drafted into the US Army, where he was commissioned through OCS. Tours of duty were spent with artillery units in Germany, Korea, and the US. While in Vietnam, he served as an adviser to a Vietnamese artillery battalion. Additionally, Kirn spent two years as an artillery instructor at the US Army Engineer School, located at Fort Belvoir, Virginia. Following his assignment to Korea, he was selected to command a joint services rest and recreation center (KMC) within the Hawaii Volcanoes National Park. The last five years of Kirn's military career were spent serving in a variety of staff assignments at Fort Polk, Louisiana. Kirn is married and has one son and one daughter. He received his baccalaureate degree from Chaminade College in Honolulu in 1971 and was awarded his master's degree from Central Michigan University before retiring as a lieutenant colonel in 1977. Additionally, he was recognized as a certified personnel consultant by the National Association of Personnel Consultants in 1991. After his retirement from the military, he worked as the executive vice president of a legal search firm, placing attorneys in law firms and corporations on a national and international scale.

www.ingramcontent.com/pod-product-compliance
Lightning Source LLC
LaVergne TN
LVHW041612070526
838199LV00052B/3108